The Courage of the Small Hours

Helen Nall

First published in Great Britain in 2010 by

Helen Nall
E-mail: fergusson.art1@btconnect.com
Website: www.fergussonsportingart.co.uk

ISBN 978-0956550002

Written and illustrated by Helen Nall.

Layout and design by Linney Group, Mansfield.

Printed in Great Britain by Linney Group.

This book is dedicated to the 55,573.

All proceeds from this book are being donated to the
R.A.F. Benevolent Fund and
The Bomber Command Memorial Appeal.

Acknowledgements

I am grateful to the following people who have displayed endless patience with my questions:

The families of the airmen who died at Hoveringham, who have kindly shared their memories with everyone reading this book.

Former Bomber Command aircrew:
Ron Brown
Roy Hill
Ron Mather
Douglas Hudson
Douglas Jennings
Joe Bell
Bill Carruthers
Jimmy James
Jim Flint

Local contributors:
Joyce Truman
George Allwood
Norman Clarke
Chris Lee
Eileen Lawton
George and Mary Hall
Jack Barnet
George Tindale
MauriceAshby

Thanks also to:
Ian Linney (Linney Group)
Tim O'Brian GAvA (Author and aviation artist)
David Needham (Author, "Nottinghamshire Air Crashes")
Brian Goulding (Author, "Lancaster at War")
Andrew Cormack (Curator of Uniforms and Medals, RAF Hendon)

and to my proof-readers, who made me work harder than I have done since A-levels:
Wing Commander (Retd.) Ron Houghton, MBE
Dr. Joel Hayward, Dean of the RAF College Cranwell
Air Commodore Ashley Stevenson OBE, Commandant RAF College Cranwell
Elizabeth Weir

…. and finally, to Ed, for not only proof-reading, but uncomplainingly taking over the shopping, school run and cooking for the past year.

INTRODUCTION

This is a story of a quiet Nottinghamshire village and some of the people who lived in and around it during the Second World War. The village is Hoveringham, my home, which is well-known as a pleasant riverside destination for day-trippers, cyclists, walkers and birdwatchers. It has been a draw for visitors since at least the nineteenth century and has not changed enormously in layout for centuries, largely because the nearby River Trent has a persistent habit of flooding from time to time. During severe floods, the waters can virtually cut off the village; Boat Lane, running from the Church to Ferry Farm, was named with good reason.

Anyone who knew the village during the war would not find it much altered now apart from the disappearance of seven working farms, two shops, the garage, an abattoir, two pubs, the school and the post office, all of which are now private homes. Hoveringham has quite naturally moved with the times in common with thousands of villages across Britain, adapting to the twenty-first century. It is now a commuter and dormitory village for Nottingham and Newark, rather than being mainly involved in agriculture. It has also gained a well-patronised sailing club, the two sailing lakes occupying what used to be riverside pasture and fields. From a distance, the sight of sails traversing what appear to be fields can be somewhat disconcerting to walkers.

This is also the story of fourteen young men who died violently within sight of our village.

Their deaths went largely unnoticed at the time as the war moved into its final stages. They were, after all, just a very few of the 55,573 Bomber Command men who lost their lives during the war.

They died in the final week of their exhaustive training as bomber aircrew. Operational squadrons and a long-awaited chance to take the war directly to the enemy awaited, but that future was abruptly denied them in the freezing darkness of the nights of 12 and 29 January 1945.

The airmen lay in silence for sixty-four years in cemeteries as far afield as Oxford and Harrogate.

On Christmas Day 2008, I received the gift of a metal detector from my husband, Edward. As I unwrapped the large upright box, half-fearing that I had been given a vacuum cleaner and wondering how I should respond if that were the case, I was unaware that my Christmas present was about to reveal tragic events from 1945.

My brother and I gave the detector its first outing on 2 January 2009. The very first sound it made was in response to a piece of metal roughly two inches in diameter with jagged, torn edges. Assuming it to be a fragment of Coca-Cola can, I was about to discard it when my brother, who happens to be a pilot, studied it more closely and pronounced it to be aircraft alloy. This was to be the first of many, many pieces of Lancaster bomber that I would find in the fields nearby. Until then, we had been unaware of the existence of an aircraft crash so close to the village. Shortly afterwards, I discovered that a lady had visited Hoveringham ten years ago in search of a memorial to her uncle, Albert Mercer, who was the Flight Engineer on Lancaster LM308. I was given her telephone number and learnt from her that, not only were Albert's sisters still alive, but that they still had no idea what had caused his aircraft to crash or even where it had come to rest.

I located and read the RAF Inquiry into the accident and felt puzzled because the official description of what happened to Albert's

Lancaster did not tally at all with what had been described to me by villagers who recalled the incident. It rapidly became apparent that there had been two Lancaster crashes in virtually the same spot. A year on and I have tracked down thirteen of the fourteen families of the crews. Having spoken with widows, girlfriends, family members and friends of the dead airmen, I felt compelled to try and build a picture of how the war began, how Hoveringham and nearby villages were affected by the conflict and how Bomber Command grew into a powerful force to be reckoned with. Finally, and maybe most of all, I wanted to explain to the families what happened to the two Lancasters and led to their relatives dying in the fields a short distance from our village.

I have learnt a lot in a brief space of time and have sometimes felt that, if I just reached out my hand, I could almost touch the face of history. With the help of Bomber Command veterans and local villagers, I realised that the world known to those airmen is really not very far behind us at all, and indeed is all too vivid in the memories of many people.

The young airmen vanished in an instant, but the fragments of metal, bullets, rivets, cockpit instruments and engine casings, scattered across the fields, represent their final moments in Lancasters JB125 and LM308.

None of this account could have happened without my brother's recognition of a shard of metal for what it was. He was an RAF pilot for many years and I think it is poignant that a chance discovery by one former RAF officer has resulted in fourteen other airmen from over six decades earlier being commemorated. Their names will be on a memorial in the pastures where they died. I like to think that this was somehow meant to be.

Chapter One

"...THIS COUNTRY IS AT WAR WITH GERMANY"

Adolf Hitler came to power in Germany in 1933 and almost immediately set about rebuilding his country's Luftwaffe, Wehrmacht and Kriegsmarine (the air force, army and navy). This re-arming directly contravened pledges made by Germany when she signed the Treaty of Versailles on 28 June 1919. It was also on a vast scale unmatched by Britain, which had coped less well with the Great Depression of 1929.

Great Britain at this time still had an empire, with India nestling beneath its imperial umbrella. At the outbreak of war in 1939, Neville Chamberlain was Prime Minister and George VI had been King for three years. Few people owned their own house or even aspired to do so. Instead, they were visited weekly by the rent man. Horses, rather than tractors, laboured with the men in the fields. Cars were a luxury for the few. Lofty and majestic elm trees still graced the landscape.

As trouble brewed across the Channel, Britain watched with mounting alarm as Hitler flaunted the terms of the Treaty. As early as 1935, following a visit to Germany, Anthony Eden, the Foreign Secretary, had reported that the extent of German re-armament dwarfed anything Britain was capable of doing. In fact, by the time war was declared, the RAF had just over 1,100 aircraft (Germany had *three* times this number), the

Navy was still employing several ships dating from the First World War and the Army had even gone so far as to disband the Tank Corps.

In 1935 Hitler reintroduced conscription – another transgression of the Versailles Treaty – and, in March the following year, he sent troops into the industrial Rhineland, despite that region being specifically designated in the Treaty as demilitarised. By the late thirties, it was apparent that he had consigned any pretence of honouring the Treaty to the long grass.

Following swiftly on the heels of these provocative actions, Hitler threatened to invade Czechoslovakia unless Britain and France supported his plans to take over the "Sudetenland", a region of Czechoslovakia bordering Germany where approximately three and a half million people spoke German and, indeed, called themselves "Germans".

Desperate to avoid war at all costs, Chamberlain met Hitler in Munich on 29 September 1938. Also present were Benito Mussolini, the Fascist Italian dictator and potential future ally for Hitler, and Édouard Daladier, the French Prime Minister and advocate of appeasement in the face of Hitler's threats. The four leaders signed the Munich Agreement at about 1.30am and Sudetenland was duly transferred to Germany on the understanding that Hitler proceeded no further into Czechoslovakia.

A weary Chamberlain returned home and the following day, 30 September, delivered his well-intentioned speech "Peace in Our Time", waving the signed agreement to the assembled crowds and film cameras. The British public was relieved and delighted at this solution and Chamberlain concluded his address by encouraging them to "go home and sleep quietly in your beds". (His hopes were to be short-lived – by March 1939, all of Czechoslovakia was under the Nazis, her army disbanded and her sophisticated arms industry seized by the German invaders.)

Britain's dismay and unease increased as the year wore on. The persecution of Jews in Germany had begun as early as spring 1933 and, between then and 1938, 25,000 German Jews had fled to Poland for sanctuary. On the night of 9 November 1938, the first large "round up" of German Jews took place in Operation "Kristallnacht". By the following summer, Jews were confined to "approved apartment blocks". This, however, was only the beginning of the horrors that were to follow.

Fearing what lay ahead, Britain churned out cheap cotton blackout material by the mile throughout 1939. It had long been assumed that the anticipated hostilities, should they materialise, would come initially from the skies. Over 30 million gas masks had been issued since the beginning of 1938. Evidence of preparations for war could be seen in other ways too: air raid siren tests, air raid precaution (ARP) exercises and intensified military activity. The RAF carried out more exercises and the number of mid-air collisions recorded across the country increased.

By mid-August 1939, war seemed inevitable and newspapers such as the *Nottingham Evening Post* blared: "War of Nerves Over Danzig – Hitler May Strike With Dramatic Suddenness". Hitler was jubilant when Stalin's Foreign Secretary, Molotov, and von Ribbentrop, his German opposite number, signed a non-aggression pact between the two countries on 24 August. (The Molotov-Ribbentrop Pact was destined to share the fate of the Versailles Treaty, being torn up by Hitler when he implemented

Operation "Barbarossa" in 1941 and invaded the Soviet Union, who had already jeopardised the treaty by invading Finland.)

In Britain, the tension continued to mount relentlessly.

The Prime Minister came home early from his holiday, returning to Downing Street on 21 August. Three days later, the King cut short his own holiday in Scotland to return to London. Sandbags appeared outside buildings of importance around the country and the clock ticked ever louder as war loomed.

By 30 August, German troops were massed and poised on the Polish border. Perhaps unsurprisingly under the circumstances, foreigners were advised to leave Poland. Despite having a huge army at their disposal, Polish commanders were confronted with the daunting task of defending 1,750 miles of border against the Reich (although the enormous land areas involved meant that Germany was also struggling cover the entire front).

In Britain, Army and RAF reservists were told to report for duty. A planned evacuation of three million children from cities began; each child carrying a gas mask and suitcase, and wearing a brown luggage label stating his or her name and home town.

Germany invaded Poland at 4.45am on 1 September. "Plan White", as it was called, had begun. The heroism of the Poles has passed into legend and, although many soldiers and civilians were killed, 100,000 managed to escape to the West and were to form the Polish Free Army under General Sikorski. (For example, 8,500 Polish pilots flew with the RAF throughout the war.) Britain and France issued an ultimatum to Germany, demanding that her forces leave Poland.

Two days later, just before 11am on Sunday 3 September, senior officers and civil servants gathered in a room in Richmond

Terrace, Whitehall, to await a message from the German Reich in which it was hoped Germany would give an assurance to withdraw her troops from Poland. A message was indeed received from the British Ambassador in Berlin, Sir Neville Henderson, but it was only to confirm that there had been no word at all from the Germans. In the minutes following this, the Secretary to the Cabinet entered the room and solemnly announced to the gathered men: "Gentlemen, we are at war with Germany". The "War Telegram" was despatched at once to various authorities.

At 11.15am, the Prime Minister broadcast this grave news to the British people, who had gathered around wireless sets across the country in readiness for his address. Everyone over a certain age recalls precisely where they were at that moment. Church services were delayed whilst the congregations listened to wirelesses instead of singing hymns. Even as the Prime Minister spoke, the first barrage balloons were being raised above Whitehall. Minutes later, the air raid sirens went off around London; a false alarm triggered by a French pilot who had not informed anyone of his route, but no less alarming for the populace.

With memories of the horrors of the Great War still fresh in people's minds, the realisation that Britain was facing the same nightmare all over again was greeted with a mixture of stunned disbelief, horror and weary resignation. There was a universal sense of needing to be at home to await further developments following Chamberlain's broadcast. Families at coastal resorts for their precious week's holiday quietly packed their things and returned home immediately; Joyce Trueman of Lowdham, near Hoveringham, was fifteen and recalls being somewhat piqued at having less than one day's holiday (three years later she would be in the Land Army).

In Hoveringham, The Old Elm Tree Inn, overlooking the River Trent, was normally bustling at weekends, but on this particular Sunday there was not a soul to be seen on the riverbank or in the pub. It seemed peculiarly paradoxical to be listening to a declaration of war on such a beautiful, sunny September morning.

The *Nottingham Evening Post* was one of the first newspapers in the country to carry the news. Its front page read "Britain at War with Germany" and, remarkably, it was on sale by midday, barely an hour after war was declared.

Thus began the "Phoney War", defined as the period between the invasion of Poland and the invasion of Denmark and Norway in April 1940, also known as the "Sitzkrieg" or, jokingly, the "Bore War". Preparations for the defence of Britain had been under way for several years and these now came fully into effect. Fear and uncertainty gripped the British population as they witnessed the brutal suppression of Poland. The nation was collectively holding its breath.

This war, however, was anything but phoney for the many who were already fighting the vicious German onslaught on the continent. Neither was it phoney for those on the high seas. U-boats had been gathering off the coast of Britain since mid-August, waiting to repeat the tactics of the First World War when convoys were targeted mercilessly, with dire effects on Britain's food supplies. (Britain had blockaded Germany's supplies in the First World War, too, with even greater success.) Only a few hours after Chamberlain's broadcast, the British liner SS Athenia, en route from Glasgow to Montreal and carrying 1,400 passengers, was torpedoed by a U-boat with the loss of 112 lives. The U-boat captain later admitted he had mistaken the liner for a merchant ship, but the nation was horrified nonetheless.

Enormous numbers of propaganda leaflets had been dropped over Germany for some time by the RAF at Chamberlain's behest in an attempt to avoid full-scale war. These leaflets were nicknamed "bomphlets" and were deposited in what was jokingly referred to by some as the "confetti war". As a matter of fact, they continued to be pushed down chutes out of aircraft throughout the war. Some officials voiced doubts about the effectiveness of bombarding the enemy with leaflets from the sky, lamenting the waste of aircrew lives and aircraft that the missions incurred. Sir Arthur Harris remained convinced that the majority of the leaflets ended up beside lavatories and should have been distributed only at the very end of the war to influence waverers, as had been done with some success in 1918. Leaflets were not going to stop the German war machine at a time when it was certain of its invincibility.

The Germans invaded Denmark and Norway in April 1940; Denmark succumbed in a matter of hours. The following month, Holland and Belgium shared the same fate and Rotterdam, whose garrison refused to withdraw, was bombed almost out of existence. It was then only a matter of time before France, too, felt the full blast of Hitler's offensive.

Hitler had drawn up plans for a fortified "line" as early as 1936, similar to those seen in the First World War. The result was the Siegfried Line, or "West Wall", which, although not completed when the war began, nonetheless managed to stretch a daunting 390 miles from the Netherlands to Weil am Rhein on the Swiss border. Manned by German soldiers and three miles deep, it was reinforced by 18,000 bunkers, tank traps and machine-gun emplacements along its length. With typical British humour, a popular song at the time was "We're Gonna Hang Out The Washing on the Siegfried Line". Defiantly facing this Siegfried Line was the equally massive French Maginot Line, likewise consisting of bunkers, machine-gun emplacements, tank traps and even an underground railway. The Maginot Line had been built from 1930 onwards with the purpose of delaying any German assault long enough to allow the French Army to mobilise. (France was suffering from a crippling shortage of young men following the devastating losses to its male population in the First World War – half of its officer corps had been killed in that conflict. This shortfall of men, combined with nervousness that a vengeful Germany might seek retribution for the humiliation of the Treaty of Versailles, had prompted construction of the Line.)

The fortifications on the Belgian border were thinly defended and did not have the tunnel network which laced the Maginot Line, as these would have been prone to flooding. There was no line whatsoever through the mountainous and dense Ardennes Forest, which was considered impassable and therefore immune from any German land assault – a disastrous miscalculation by the French. It was perfectly logical for the Germans to mount their attack across the weaker Belgian defences and through the Ardennes Forest, which they did successfully and with tremendous speed. Hardly surprisingly, the Luftwaffe simply flew straight over the French defences.

At this time, Hitler was still heeding the advice of his military commanders and was in turn respected by them (he had, after all, twice been awarded the Iron Cross in the First World War); this happy balance, however, was not destined to last the course of the war.

Suffering from a lack of money and preparation, the French Air Force had no modern aircraft ready for service. An agreement between France and Britain had led to the formation of the RAF Advanced Air Striking Force (AASF) on 24 August 1939. This bomber force was despatched to France, arriving by September to support the British Expeditionary Force, which had an Air Component of fighters for defence of ground forces. British bomber squadrons based in France were duly instructed to attack German tactical targets such as convoys, lorries, tanks and bridges, and strategic targets such factories.

The Battle of France only lasted a few weeks but bomber crew losses during that time were appalling. The average survival rate for an airman was nine raids. The Defiant, with a crew of two and a powered gun turret (but no forward firing gun) was no match for the superior Luftwaffe Messerschmitt fighters and suffered heavy casualties. The Battles and Blenheims fared no better and many young men perished in these outdated aircraft. The first two air VCs awarded in the war went (posthumously) to the crew of a Fairey Battle which, hit by enemy fire on a bombing approach to destroy a bridge, deliberately aimed their stricken aircraft at the bridge spars. They destroyed the bridge but lost their lives.

Spitfires had been posted to the Continent as part of the Air Component. They did not cope well with the uneven grass airfields in France and were pulled back to Britain, but not before a sizeable number of them had unfortunately "crunched" when taking off or landing. The wheels being positioned very close to each other (the undercarriage retracted outwards) rendered them notoriously unstable if they encountered a rabbit hole or other obstacle and they were also regarded as tricky customers to land in crosswinds. The Hurricane's wheels were set wider apart (they retracted inwards) and it was rather more stable when taking off and landing, coping better with the rough French airstrips.

As the Germans advanced, the French Premier, Paul Reynaud, pleaded with Churchill for a further ten British fighter squadrons to be deployed to France, a request doggedly and wisely opposed by the head of Fighter Command, Air Chief Marshal Sir Hugh (later Lord) Dowding. It was clear to him that the cause in France was lost and that his scant resources – particularly his precious Spitfires – needed to be husbanded for the inevitable Luftwaffe onslaught on Britain. Churchill was initially keen to despatch the ten squadrons of fighters to defend France, but had not reckoned on Dowding's stubborn nature. The fighters remained in Britain.

The AASF played a valiant part in attempting to defend France. There were, however, regular disputes between the French and the British about what the bombers' targets should be. The British refused or ignored the more unpractical – and sometimes downright fantastic – French requests for bombardment, which led to major disagreements. With classic British understatement, Bomber Harris recalls the bombing campaign of the Battle of France as being somewhat "muddled".

The approaching Germans and the imminent fall of France meant squadrons were ordered to return to England. There are accounts of the German bombers attacking aerodromes from which British aircraft had fled minutes before; the helpless ground crews left behind were often not as fortunate in escaping the German bombs.

Chamberlain resigned as Prime Minister on 13 May, following a disastrous campaign in Norway and pressure from Labour members seeking a more proactive response to Germany. Winston Churchill became the head of the wartime coalition government.

From 27 May 1940, the soldiers of the British Expeditionary Force – which had been defeated – were evacuated from the beaches of Dunkirk. The pursuing German army had inexplicably been ordered to stop twenty miles from where its prey – virtually the entire British Army – was pinned on the beaches. This pause enabled 338,000 men to escape to Britain. Amongst the men rescued were tens of thousands of French soldiers, many of whom would go on to form the core of the Free French Army under General de Gaulle.

The exhausted troops stood in snaking lines on the beaches, often chest-deep in water, patiently awaiting salvation whilst enduring merciless dive-bombing and strafing from screaming Stukas. (My great-uncle was a stretcher-bearer; the man on the stretcher was killed when they were raked by fire from a strafing German plane. My great-uncle was eventually rescued but subsequently died, aged 21, from pneumonia following his prolonged immersion in the Channel.) Aside from the Navy's vessels, many of the flotilla of boats which crossed the Channel to rescue these men were tiny pleasure craft and fishing boats, manned by truly courageous civilians (some still teenagers), in what was named "Operation Dynamo". The events leading up to Dunkirk unquestionably marked a crushing defeat for the British Army but, if proof were required to show how the British people could rally, the world needed to look no further than the evacuation which followed. Dunkirk remains one of our defining moments of history and a source of national pride.

Bomber Command sent Blenheims, Hampdens, Wellingtons and what few Fairey Battles were still airworthy in France to attack the enemy and to endeavour to help the men on the beaches. Coastal Command played its part and Fighter Command flew 2,739 sorties to take on the Stukas, losing 106 fighters and with 75 pilots killed or taken prisoner. The RAF lost a great many aircraft, but heavy cloud cover and smoke over the French coast meant that the air battles were not visible to the soldiers below, many of whom later accused the Air Force of abandoning them to the Luftwaffe. "Where was the RAF?" was commonly asked and there were accounts of airmen being jeered by soldiers back in England.

France fell and Hitler insisted that the Armistice document be signed in the very same railway carriage at Verdun that had witnessed the German signing of the Armistice in November 1918. To make his point, he then ordered the carriage be blown up so that it could never be used again.

The cinemas in Britain were crammed as people awaited the latest Pathé newsreels to see how the war was going; they filled the aisles and every possible space. The newsreels were days old, having had to be transported from the battlefields. Watching the images of Dunkirk and of British troops returning home defeated, the mood was sombre and many were privately convinced the war was lost. The army was exhausted and, to compound the calamity, most of its heavy armaments had had to be abandoned on the French beaches.

It was a desperately low point in the war and, despite Winston Churchill's morale-raising speeches, the English Channel suddenly seemed terrifyingly narrow, and the British Isles tiny. The spring of 1940 is remembered as a particularly warm one, but the icy chill from events across the Channel was to be felt on our shores before long.

The so-called phoney war was over.

Chapter Two

BRITAIN PUTS UP HER FISTS

In 1939, the fear of invasion gripped Britain. People were intensely suspicious of strangers in pubs, shops, clubs, and even doctors' waiting rooms in case the enemy had infiltrated their community. Defensive structures and organisations appeared across the country. Some are still visible today, seamlessly absorbed into our landscape. A squat pillbox by a river is as much a part of our heritage now as any medieval castle. The protection of the civilian population from the Luftwaffe was paramount, so air raid shelters of various designs were constructed in tremendous numbers in the run up to, and after the outbreak of, hostilities.

The best-known kind of air raid shelter was the Anderson shelter, named after Sir John Anderson, the Secretary of State for Home Affairs. Initially these shelters were available at no cost, particularly to town dwellers: two million of them had been supplied by September 1939. By March 1940, when steel stocks were dwindling, anyone earning over a certain amount was required to pay for their shelter. Consisting of two sheets of corrugated steel bolted together at the top to form a curved roof, they were fairly easy to construct, and were intended to be placed at the end of gardens, embedded three feet into the ground with eighteen inches of earth or turfs covering the roof. They could hold up to six people and, whilst they would not have withstood a direct hit from a bomb, they gave families a greater sense of security and provided some protection from bomb debris and red-hot shrapnel falling from exploding anti-aircraft shells. Over 24,000 Anderson shelters were distributed throughout Nottingham city alone. One family hastened to their Anderson shelter during a raid on Nottingham only to find the elderly grandmother had not emerged from the house. Her son ran back inside and found her searching for her false teeth. He grabbed her arm and led her outside to the shelter, saying: "Mother, it's bombs they're dropping, not ham sandwiches!"

Some families built their own air raid shelters out of brick. Others relied on communal shelters which could hold up to fifty people: these had benches around the walls but it was the awful damp smell that appears to be the primary recollection. Factories, hospitals, railway stations and schools frequently had their own air raid shelters. Kitty Foster attended Epperstone School, three miles from Hoveringham, and remembers watching her father and other parents in the village digging a zig-zag air raid trench for the children in a field across the road from the school.

People without access to a garden, as well as disabled or very elderly people, received indoor "Morrison" shelters. These were made of steel and resembled a cage beneath a sturdy table; they had to be crawled into. (My great-grandmother used to sit in her Morrison shelter in North-East England during air raids, and once she was safely in, she would complete her protection against the Luftwaffe by solemnly placing a tea-cosy on her head.) In the absence of a shelter, basements were the next best thing.

The official advice to people if attacked by German bombers was: "On no account look out of the window during an air raid". You

could be forgiven for thinking this to be self-evident, yet one ARP
Warden recalls: "There was always some idiot who wanted to
stand outside and watch the bombs fall".

Gas masks had to be carried at all times and children's masks
were made of coloured rubber, rather than black, to make them
less intimidating to youngsters. Alan Yates attended Lowdham
School as a child and remembers the entire class walking around
the classroom wearing their gasmasks, as part of a practice.

To make navigation difficult for the Germans, had they invaded,
road signs, village names and railway station name boards
were removed (this inevitably confounded the British populace,
too). Ironically, at the end of hostilities, POWs were frequently
employed in the restoration of these signs.

The War Office appealed to builders, farmers and garage owners
to come forward and contact their local Town Clerk with offers of
suitable obstacles which could be used to obstruct potential landing
grounds and prevent enemy aircraft or gliders from landing. Items
had to be "substantial and heavy" and "old wagons, lorries, heavy
poles and timbers, bricks and rubble, large pipes, trees and farm
implements" were sought after in particular.

As a result of this request, poles were erected in flat fields. They
resembled telegraph poles and were on average twelve to fifteen
feet high. Farmers in Hoveringham and Thurgarton were paid a
shilling per pole, per annum, as compensation for having their land
festooned. The poles in the Hoveringham pastures adjacent to the
Old Elm Tree Inn are vividly recalled by many people. They were
simply part of the landscape. (The first of the two Lancasters which
crashed in this pasture in 1945 missed one of these poles by inches,
only to come to grief a short distance further on in the next field.)

To reassure the public in 1939, the Ministry of Information and the War Office issued a torrent of leaflets which were pushed through letterboxes with advice covering subjects such as how to reinforce windows against bomb-splinters and how to comply with the blackout. One of the better-known leaflets was entitled *"If the Invader comes..."* and amongst its rather terse instructions were:

Do not give the German anything.

Hide food and bicycles.

Hide maps.

See that the enemy gets no petrol.

To a certain extent, the advice on what to do in the event of a German invasion depended on individual circumstances. Angela Nall's school had been evacuated in 1940 from the north Kent coast to the comparative safety of Gloucestershire. The girls received precise instructions from their Headmistress, Miss Gammell, about what to do in the event of German paratroopers appearing out of the skies. They should curl into a ball on the ground and fling their green skirts over their heads, which would conceal their white blouses from above. As the girls' uniform fortuitously included matching green knickers, their camouflage was complete.

One of the most visual deterrents to the enemy were barrage balloons. The civilian population found the presence of these blimps reassuring and they were certainly treated with respect by pilots on both sides.

First used in 1917, by 1936, 450 balloons had been approved to defend London from future attacks and Balloon Command was officially formed on 1 November 1938. In 1939, there were 47 Barrage Balloon squadrons and, by 1942, about 10,000 balloon operators had been trained. The only snag was that they were nearly all men and as the war progressed, they were required on the Front Line. The suggestion that women could perfectly well operate the balloons to "free up" the men proved unpopular with AOC Balloon Command. Nonetheless, by 1942 the 10,000 men had been replaced by 15,700 women and, by 1943, the balloons were being operated almost entirely by these members of the Women's Auxilliary Air Force (WAAFs).

Balloons were to be found around important facilities and afforded a good degree of protection by forcing enemy aircraft to fly higher and into the range of the anti-aircraft guns. The balloon and cable were not the real threat to an aircraft. They were merely a means of suspending a mine (attached to the cable) which would cause the actual damage. Should an aircraft fly into the cable, it would break off below the balloon, which then drifted away, its job done. A small parachute on one end of the cable – which would, by now, be snagged across the wing – filled with air and drew the remaining length of cable and its mine over the wing. The mine exploded on contact with the leading edge of the wing and no aircraft could withstand such damage. (Lancasters had wire cutters on the leading edge of their wings to counter the danger of barrage balloons.)

The balloon was manned around the clock. WAAFs operated in teams of eight to a balloon and lived in a Nissen hut. They were self-sufficient and did two hours on duty, then four hours off. Each member of the team was provided with a torch, a whistle and a truncheon for protection against the Germans. The huts were freezing in winter when the girls would pull their beds end-on to the brazier in the centre of the hut. Judy Brown of Newark, was a WAAF working as part of a balloon unit, and recalls earwigs being a particular problem, getting tangled in the girls' hair during the night and having to be shaken out of their gasmasks in the mornings.

The balloon was attached to a Ford V8 truck cab (minus wheels) with a winch attached to it to wind the balloon in and out. Concrete blocks helped anchor the balloon and the girls turned the balloon into the prevailing wind direction. There were four flexible steel cables on either side of the balloon for them all to hang on to and it was very hard, physical work, often in appalling weather conditions. The balloons were made of rubber-proofed cotton, over 60 feet long and 30 feet high and weighing about 550lb when inflated. All repairs to the balloon were carried out by the WAAFs who had to wear special shoes with soft soles so that they could climb inside without damaging the fabric (some of the girls refused point-blank to go inside them). Lorries delivered the hydrogen gas. The WAAFs "bedded down" the balloons at night. If they were called out in the night by Balloon Command to fly the balloon, the WAAFs would stumble around half-awake in the dark in their pyjamas. The area immediately around the balloon was protected by an eighteen inch high perimeter wire which was tripped over (and cursed) countless times. Judy recalls being shouted at by the others as she had fallen asleep hanging onto her wire, only letting go seconds before the balloon was raised.

These enormous blimps could tear themselves free from their moorings in strong winds. One balloon was recorded as travelling as far from mainland England as Jersey and many more ended up in other surprise destinations. The Hoveringham Home Guard had to investigate what was at first thought to be a solitary German paratrooper caught in an oak tree in Station Road between Thurgarton and Hoveringham; closer inspection in the moonlight revealed the intruder to be a deflated barrage balloon which had broken free from Derby and become ensnared in the branches.

The day after Holland surrendered on 14 May 1940, the War Minister, Anthony Eden, made a BBC broadcast, the result of which was the creation of an immense civilian army which remains a source of national pride, and a little popular humour through "Dad's Army", to this day. The Home Guard was about to make its appearance.

The situation of the country was so dire that Eden appealed directly to all British men aged 17 – 65 to "come forward and offer their services". The organisation was to be called the Local Defence Volunteers – swiftly nicknamed "Look, Duck and Vanish" by wags. The purpose of this new force was very clear: to report on the enemy's advance, and to be a wholehearted nuisance to them until the Regular Army turned up.

Within twenty-four hours of Eden's broadcast, a quarter of a million men had enrolled, rising to one and a half million by the end of the first month. The LDV presented an opportunity for boys and men to contribute to the war effort in the nearest form of military service many of them were likely to see. Boys still too young to be in the Regular Army but who were obviously young men, could at last hold their heads up before those who accused them of dodging service. Many of those who enlisted were in reserved occupations; farm labourers, for instance – who wished to do more for the defence of Britain. A large proportion of the men who initially came forward were First World War veterans in their forties, but by 1943 the average age of the volunteers had fallen to 30.

Men began to present themselves at police stations, as instructed, from the moment Eden finished his broadcast. Queues rapidly formed and the police, who had not been well-briefed about this momentous decision by the Government, felt totally overwhelmed in some areas by the sheer numbers gathering outside their station doors. Somehow, though, the names of the volunteers were taken down by the police officers and the men were sworn in as members of the Local Defence Volunteers: some on the spot, others a few days later. What they all shared was an iron resolve to stand up and defend Britain, with whatever weapons they had to hand.

So many men volunteered that was impossible to provide them all with uniforms immediately, so they initially wore armbands with the letters LDV to identify themselves. An interesting array of weaponry began to appear, frequently found in attics and dusted off from previous wars. An elephant gun, produced by one volunteer, must have raised eyebrows, but to the owner it was evidently better than the pitchforks, hedge stakes, sticks, rifles and shotguns brandished by most of the men. Jokes abounded: one volunteer wanted to know if a licence was required for shooting German paratroopers during the "parachutist season".

The Hoveringham and Thurgarton LDV counted butchers, farmers and a head gardener amongst its numbers. Not everyone, however, was in a position to enlist in the LDV. John Knowles lived near Hoveringham and recalls his father going to the local Labour Exchange to explain why he would not be an ideal candidate (he had lost his right leg at Ypres in the First World War, which most people would have judged an adequate excuse).

The official repeatedly asked for Knowles to present proof of exemption from his doctor, whereupon, in exasperation, Knowles raised and dropped the wooden leg onto the table. The matter was not pursued.

There was a great deal for the LDV to defend. Gasworks, railway stations, power sub-stations, bridges and waterways were all potential targets for the Germans. 20,000 miles of railway line, the life-blood of the country and vital for moving supplies, troops and fuel around, needed round-the-clock protection.

Roadblocks were erected by the LDV to check identity cards and also to impede the Germans if they came. These obstructions were constructed from whatever could be spared: old furniture, planks, and sandbags featuring large. The volunteers were instructed to shoot at people who failed to stop and more than one driver was killed as a consequence; short-sightedness on the part of the motorist being a factor in several incidents.

The LDV commandeered church towers as observation platforms. The Government constructed concrete pill-boxes across the country to defend important sites, although they were not manned all the time and were more often than not used as stores for the LDV. They were usually made of concrete, with variations in design depending on location and purpose. Most had a sturdy door and slit apertures to shoot through (I often played in pillboxes in Hertfordshire as a child: they were freezing cold, damp and exceedingly claustrophobic, but once the door was closed they were secure and absolutely no one else could get in.)

At the end of June 1940, Churchill suggested that the name of the LDV be changed to the Home Guard. Ranks mirroring those of the Regular Army were also introduced, meaning that "Volunteer

Smith" became "Private Smith", and so on. Despite this official recognition of their contribution, all Home Guard officers were still instructed by the War Office to travel third class on railways to reduce costs: their comfort was less important than the nation's defence.

By the time of the Battle of Britain, the Home Guard volunteers had their uniforms and weapons to arm them were arriving in large numbers from the United States. (Roosevelt was keen to support the Allies as much as he could without relinquishing America's neutrality; there was great opposition amongst Americans to joining the war in Europe.)

The men of the Home Guard learned aircraft recognition, mine-laying, field-craft and guerrilla warfare, map-reading and First Aid. They learned how to make petrol bombs and to strip and clean guns, the aim being to produce fighters who would be a thorough and effective irritant to the invading Germans and hinder their advance. Training manuals were issued by the War Office, as well as leaflets listing useful German phrases. As the war progressed, the Home Guard proved itself very useful in freeing the regular army from tasks such as manning anti-aircraft guns. the Home Guard were overnight sensations in Scotland in 1941, when Rudolph Hess, Hitler's Deputy, flew himself to Britain to offer his services as a mediator between Britain and Germany. The first person to come across Hess was David McLean, a Scottish farm worker and member of his local Home Guard unit.

The Home Guard in Hoveringham frequently gathered in the waiting room at Thurgarton station; the main reason – according to many villagers – was not because the Germans were expected to appear on the train from Lincoln, but because the waiting room had a warm fire. One of the Home Guard mislaid a round of ammunition overnight; the following morning the station master inadvertently swept it up and, as the sweepings were hurled on the fire, it went off up the chimney.

The Hoveringham unit formed up on one occasion outside the church and proceeded to march along Main Street before left-wheeling into the cricket club grounds. To the delight of the young boys watching, the men mounted a practice assault on the pavilion from behind, forcing their way noisily through a high hedge and enthusiastically throwing thunder-flashes.

Some Home Guard units based in hilly, moor land or mountainous regions took to the saddle, horses enabling the men to access remote areas otherwise unreachable by foot patrols or vehicles. North Yorkshire, Wales, Dartmoor and Exmoor were amongst the regions covered by patrols mounted on horses. Many of the men were erstwhile foxhunters, German paratroopers having been substituted for foxes. The Flintham Home Guard unit, tasked with protecting RAF Syerston and its environs, included a mounted group of men who patrolled the Trent hills which loom above Hoveringham.

The River Trent had its own River Patrol. This waterborne unit of the Home Guard covered almost 100 miles of the river, including the stretch which passes between Syerston and Hoveringham. The patrol was based at Gunthorpe, where the Army was fully prepared to destroy the bridge with mines in the event of a German invasion.

Seventeen-year-old Herbert Rylatt joined the Home Guard at Flintham in 1940 and helped the Army to guard RAF Syerston. He notes that he and the other men had "no uniform, but two rifles" and enjoyed the dubious luxury of a bell tent with a groundsheet in the pouring rain. They were permitted a brazier which they stuffed with soggy twigs but, as they were not allowed to show any light, the brazier never really heated up and consequently the tea was truly awful, having been made with "smoky, tepid water". He was understandably relieved to be called up to the Regular Army the following year.

By the time the Home Guard stood down on Sunday 3 December 1944, nearly two million men had served in its ranks. The stand down was marked by parades and ceremonies countrywide (Newark held one in the Market Square). Those men who stepped forward to join the Home Guard were the most patriotic of volunteers, regularly undertaking the extra hours of duty on top of full-time employment elsewhere. Often mocked by Regular soldiers, as well as some members of the public, over time their courage and grim determination to see off the Germans earned profound admiration from all quarters.

The Royal Observer Corps was another voluntary organisation which played a major role in the war. The Corps was originally set up in 1914 to report to the Admiralty on aircraft and airships seen within sixty miles of London. Observation posts were constructed between the wars in England, Scotland and Wales. Each post had a theodolite, binoculars and telephone, and the men manning the post would record the altitude and speed of all enemy aircraft that crossed the British coastline. In 1939, the Corps, then comprising around 10,000 volunteers, many of whom were men too old to be on active service, was mobilised by Fighter Command. The Corps proved itself so effective at tracking aircraft during the Battle of Britain in 1940 that George VI afterwards conferred the title

"Royal" upon it. The renamed Royal Observer Corps saw large numbers of WAAFs transferred to its ranks shortly afterwards, and male staff at its headquarters, RAF Bentley Priory, were compulsorily retired at the age of fifty (which proved far from popular with many amongst them.) The age limit did not apply to men manning posts, many of whom were in their seventies and even eighties! Thereafter, the Corps was employed in tracking the enormous numbers of aircraft – both enemy and allied – in the air at any time. During the course of the war, its role was expanded to include assisting the Air Force by guiding RAF planes to safety, particularly in bad weather.

The local unit covering Hoveringham had its base at Lowdham and its lookout post was at Hill Crest (now Hill House), a spectacular vantage point with uninterrupted views of the Trent Valley for many miles in either direction. RAF Syerston is located at a similar height a few miles away, straight across the valley, and its massive hangars are clearly visible. The men of the Lowdham unit were administered by Mr. Barker, the Headmaster of Lowdham School, who was not keen at all on the stiff walk up the hill to the post.

As the war intensified, the British grew accustomed to living in darkness. The blackout was rigorously enforced and observed. The shout of "You're showing a light!" from the ARP Warden has passed into lore and stiff fines were handed out to miscreants by magistrates. The Air Raid Precautions warden in Hoveringham lived at Lindum Cottage and a sign with the letters "ARP" was displayed prominently on the gate. Some families, terrified of the Luftwaffe, went so far as to make sure there was nothing pale such as bits of paper or litter outside their houses which might draw the enemy's attention.

People blundered around in darkened streets and tripped over unexpected obstacles like sandbags and lamp-posts, with the famous British pea-soup fogs adding to the difficulties in winter. Britons visiting America, Canada and South Africa were invariably awe-struck by the fact that "all the lights were on" in those countries.

Bicycles had swiftly become the sole means of transport for many civilians. However, riding a bicycle in the blackout with only a feeble light was challenging to say the least, and the risk of collision with other road-users and static objects was significantly increased. Bicycles were permitted one small, hooded lamp. A fine of ten shillings was imposed for not displaying a light. Yet, as the war continued, batteries for torches and lights were so scarce that dynamos became much sought-after. Bicycles were indispensable to RAF personnel for getting around the enormous airfields (and also for getting from pub to pub in the local villages).

To comply with the blackout, all motorised vehicles had to affix half-moon shaped covers over their headlights. A narrow horizontal strip of light – about 3 by 1 inches – was all that was permitted.

Wartime regulations meant that bus roofs were painted khaki and leading edges of bodywork painted white. They had similarly masked headlamps, and on occasion, particularly in thick fog, the conductors would be required to sit on the engine hood and shine a torch at the verge for the driver to use as a guide as they crept along. This was not always a successful remedy and one local bus with a full load of passengers en route from Nottingham to Newark had been glued to the tail-lights of the vehicle in front of it, which were just discernable in the murk. The car that it had been following pulled into a driveway in Elston and its driver, who was merely returning home from his job in Nottingham, was surprised to find that not only the bus but about twenty other vehicles had followed him blindly to his front door. Chaos ensued as each vehicle had to reverse and be directed back to the Fosse.

Buses and trams had blinds on their windows, and blue lights were the only interior illumination, making passengers assume an unnatural glow. Counting change, when you could barely see your hand in front of your face, was no mean feat for the conductor. These eerie blue lights were also used in the trucks ferrying aircrew to their waiting Lancasters before a raid.

Perhaps unsurprisingly, pedestrian deaths in Britain tripled to over 550 between August and September 1939. A speed limit of 30 mph was advised on main roads and a very cautious 15 mph on narrow lanes. In Newark, kerbstones were painted a chequerboard white pattern to assist pedestrians and motorists alike. Trees in the town sported white rings around their girth and mudguards on cars were likewise painted white. Some men left their shirt-tails hanging out to make them more visible to vehicles approaching from behind. Horses in the Hoveringham area were at least spared the fate of the free-roaming New Forest ponies in the south of the country: a number of those creatures had white bands painted on them which can only have added to the air of surrealism.

Farmers were forbidden from transporting hay and straw after dark as these were deemed to be on the list of inflammable products which were banned from public roads at night. The Old Elm Tree Inn at Hoveringham, thronged with airmen from RAF Syerston, had a large glass kitchen roof and it fell to Eileen Lawton, being the smallest in the landlord's family, to clamber precariously out of an upstairs window at dusk and unroll an old length of carpet to cover the glass for the blackout, a feat that then had to be repeated in the morning to remove it.

Churches posed a blackout headache, although the authorities did concede that it would be nigh on impossible to black out every single pane of church glass. As a compromise, Sunday evening services were brought forward to 3pm in the winter.

Nor were trains exempt from the blackout: Ernest Witney was a driver's mate on the railways and was based at Colwick, one of the largest marshalling yards in the country. If German bombers were known to be approaching, a signalman waved an orange lamp to order drivers to shut the steam off and apply the brakes. As the train slowed, a paraffin lamp with purple shades confirmed the air raid and a tarpaulin was draped over the entire cab to hide the glow of the firebox from the enemy aircraft overhead. The heat in the cab, once a tarpaulin was in place, was hellish. A speed limit of 15 mph was also imposed, to lessen the risk of giveaway sparks being emitted from the funnel.

In the last few months of the war, the Government reduced the blackout to the "dim-out" as the threat from Germany lessened. People began to hit upon innovative uses for redundant blackout material; one inspired lady from Harby, a few miles from Hoveringham, used her blackout curtains to make football shorts for the entire village team. (Further afield, at Cheltenham Ladies College in 1947, they used theirs to make robes for the chorus, the old men of Thebes, in the school production of "Antigone"!)

As well as adapting to a life of murky darkness, the British learned what hunger meant. Many people had unpleasant memories stirred of the near-disaster of 1917, when, with Britain's men away fighting and many of the working horses also commandeered by the Army, the country had been three weeks away from completely running out of food reserves. The German Navy had succeeded in blockading Britain's food imports, which comprised half of the country's food requirements (although Britain had imposed her own highly effective naval blockades on Germany, too). To complete the nightmare, the harvest had failed that year.

Chamberlain had been a member of the Cabinet in the First World War and had witnessed at first-hand the effect of enemy blockades and resulting food crisis of 1917, so it seems incomprehensible that Britain's dependence upon imported food had been allowed to grow to the proportions it had reached by 1939. At the outbreak of the Second World War, Britain imported over sixty per cent of her food.

To avoid a repeat of that scenario, ration books were introduced in 1939, petrol being the first commodity to be regulated, and they remained part of life in Britain until 1954. Bacon, butter and sugar were the first food items to be rationed (in January 1940), followed before long by meat, tea, jam, cheese, eggs, rice, tinned tomatoes, peas, sweets, chocolate and biscuits. Game was not rationed. The Ministry of Food constantly issued imaginative recipes to reflect the reduced availability of food whilst encouraging the population to maintain a balanced diet.

Some individuals found a way around the rations: a worker at the abattoir in Nottingham regularly smuggled back to Hoveringham cuts of meat concealed in his lunch bag. As he cycled to the city and back every day it can be assumed that a substantial quantity of meat found its way to Hoveringham residents over the years. Others relied on poaching to supplement the meat diet. Bernard Mayo worked at Hoveringham Gravel and his daughter Barbara watched him at their home, Rose Cottage, making nets to trap rabbits. Generally, it was easier to source food in the more rural areas of Britain; gardens could be dug up and planted with vegetables, and chickens could be kept. Kitty Foster lived in Epperstone, four miles from Hoveringham, and maintains her family were never hungry during the war, unlike some town-dwellers. Households could keep one pig which was fed on kitchen scraps and slaughtered annually. The fat would be taken off the carcass and rendered down, the small intestines were used to make sausages, and the bladder made a half-decent football. The meat would be dry-salted and stored. (One family in Kneeton always had an extra, illicit slaughtered pig hung on the back of the pantry door, which was swiftly closed whenever officials appeared.)

John Embling was a young boy in Kneeton during the war and recalls his staple wartime diet as comprising primarily bread, jam and cheese. Any meat at all was a treat and rabbits were a welcome addition to the Embling family table. At harvest time, John and other boys from the village would pursue bolting rabbits and try to "clobber" them with a big stick. His mother would ask him to find a "hump-backed" rabbit to make the pie look fuller under the crust. Another family in Kneeton kept rabbits specifically for food and were concerned by the extreme pinkness of the animals' flesh, the mystery eventually being solved when it was discovered that the creatures had inexplicably been fed a diet of beetroots.

Bees were kept by Lady Nall at Hoveringham Hall, as they were by many householders, the honey being a perfect substitute for sugar. Another resourceful, but misguided, lady spent an entire afternoon (doomed to failure) attempting to extract sugar from a single sugar beet.

The Hoveringham Parish Council noted in September 1940 that any surplus fruit was to be "reported to the Miss Armitage who has control of fruit for jam-making in the district".

Clothing was rationed to the equivalent of one new whole outfit per year. Uniforms were utilitarian and one local WAAF recalls being issued with black or navy knickers, which were nicknamed "passion killers". They were, she said: "like the harvest. All was safely gathered in." Furniture was also rationed, only being available to those setting up home for the first time, or to those who had been bombed and had lost their possessions.

Coal and soap were rationed and people were urged not to waste water. I recall being perplexed as a small child in the early 1970s, as my grandmother ran what seemed to be the shallowest of baths with barely room for my toys. Thirty years after the war, she still adhered to the recommended five inches of water for a bath.

Towns had bins at the end of each street to collect waste food and scraps. (Alan Yates lived in Mansfield during the war and found, that by rummaging through these bins, he sourced enough scraps to feed his few chickens.) The scraps went off to be turned into what was commonly nicknamed "Tottenham Pudding" for pigs.

It was painfully apparent, as war loomed, that Britain was rapidly going to have to learn how to feed herself – and that meant growing much, much more food than she had been doing.

To this end, between May and September 1939, the War Agricultural Committee (or "War Ag" as it was swiftly nicknamed) directed farmers to plough up their pasture and meadows to grow additional food in what became known as the "Battle for Wheat". The aim was to plough up two million acres of land, particularly grassland, in time for the 1940 harvest and this target was successfully reached by April 1940. (A further five million acres were to be ploughed up by the end of the war.) The loss of pasture, however, was resisted and resented by dairy farmers in particular, who felt that milk production was being sidelined. Epperstone cricket pitch and tennis courts were sacrificed for this purpose, to the distress of the two elderly groundsmen. "It was sacrilege", recalls John Knowles, who witnessed the destruction as a boy. Local War Agricultural Committees inspected farms to ensure the land was being adequately used.

In the fields around Hoveringham, a fiendish machine made its terrifying appearance to add its weight to the war effort. It was called a Gyrotiller and a more unearthly creation it would hard to imagine. Made by John Fowler of Leeds, these machines had first been produced in 1927. This contraption, of which there were several versions, was diesel-powered and ran on tracks like a tank. It is perhaps best described as a cross between a steam traction engine and a modern food blender; its powerful rotating blades made mincemeat of the old hedgerows and thickets. It levelled, and simultaneously ploughed, the uneven old pastures between Hoveringham and Thurgarton to prepare them for cultivation. These monsters could work twenty-four hours a day if necessary and were operated across the country by contractors during the war. The local contractor for Hoveringham, Epperstone and Thurgarton was called George; he lived in a small caravan which he towed behind his Gyrotiller as he travelled from job to job.

But undoubtedly the most remarkable contribution to food production was the formation of the Women's Land Army. The WLA originally appeared in Britain's fields during the First World War in response to the looming food crisis, and by 1918, there were 23,000 Land Girls milking, ploughing and tending the herds. The WLA was disbanded in 1919 as the men returned from the war and food shipments resumed from overseas.

In 1939, the redoubtable Lady Denman oversaw the re-forming of the WLA. She had to contend with scorn and derision from farmers who felt that the land was no place for women (yet it was the National Farmers' Union who voiced the loudest support for the WLA when it was finally disbanded in 1950). Suspicion amongst farmers and male labourers that this was a ruse to introduce cheap labour to the countryside and undercut existing wages led to the Union of Agricultural Workers at first refusing to countenance the prospect of girls on the land.

Thousands of women applied to join the Land Army, enticed by posters of glamorous girls effortlessly carrying sheaves of corn whilst flashing a beaming smile. Girls aged seventeen and over were eligible to join, although there were incidents of younger girls signing up, background checks being fairly rudimentary. They were interviewed and underwent a medical inspection; some conditions, such as short-sightedness were brushed aside. One myopic girl who struggled to read the letters on the board during an eyesight test was told by the doctor that he would sign her as fit for duty, as no doubt she would "see a charging bull".

Eventually, but with no thanks to the Ministry of Agriculture which dragged its feet at every opportunity, the local WLA committees proposed by Lady Denman were approved and set up – a whole year after she was appointed head of the WLA and only days before the outbreak of war. Miraculously, the first two groups of Land Girls completed their training before September 1939 in readiness to combat the estimated shortfall of 50,000 agricultural workers that had been lost over the previous decades to factories or into the armed forces.

Each Land Girl had two identical uniforms of khaki-coloured corduroy breeches and shirts, and a green jumper. The breeches were nicknamed "whistling" breeches by some Girls because of the noise the fabric made as they walked. Wellington boots and overalls were provided for field work and an overcoat for smart wear. After the fall of Malaya in 1941, rubber imports plummeted, leading to a chronic shortage of Wellington boots; as a result only Land Girls working in dairy farms were issued with them.

Over a third of Land Girls hailed from London and the northern industrial cities: a more alien working environment for barmaids, hairdressers, shop-girls, mill-workers and recent schoolgirls than the countryside – especially in winter – is hard to imagine. Their wages were about 30 shillings a week, with board and lodgings deducted from that. There was no set holiday period; this was decided by the individual farmers.

The hours were long: 48 hours a week in winter and 50 in summer, although the harvest entailed much longer days and 50 hours a week would then be purely theoretical (the same long hours still apply during harvest-time today). The Girls cycled to whichever farm they had been allocated to in the vicinity, leaving the hostel at 7.30 am with a packed lunch. Those girls near RAF Syerston worked until Saturday lunchtime and went home if possible, using Mr. Gash's bus along the Fosse Way into Newark, hitching lifts or walking if no transport was available.

Each Land Girl received the "Land Army Manual", containing advice on their new lifestyles but, as many Girls were placed singly on farms, it could be a lonely occupation and not every girl recalls her time as a Land Girl fondly. Some of the farmers are remembered as ogres who made the Girls' lives a misery; others say these years were the best of their lives.

The foreman at the Boots farm at Thurgarton, near Hoveringham, was profuse in his praise of the Land Girls helping to operate the threshing machine, renowned as a notoriously testing task. Another local farmer however, is remembered as being impossible to please and was readily incensed by the Girls' frequent giggling fits (which invariably led to more giggling). It was simply the luck of the draw for the Girls.

Farm machinery had been designed with male operators in mind and the work was physically very demanding. The Girls tended herds, milked, ploughed, spread muck and picked potatoes, peas, carrots and beet. (The Girls lifted the beet and lay them on their sides, returning later with a knife to "top" them. Irish labourers, though, had a rather slick "lift them and top them all-in-one-motion" system, which meant they finished a field long before anyone else.) No farm job was outside their remit; about a thousand Land Girls were trained as rat-catchers.

Yet the Girls suffered appalling prejudice from many quarters. Many had given up far better-paid jobs to join the WLA and so, in effect, took large pay cuts to do their "duty"; many felt exploited by the system. Some were given no hot meals throughout the winter months, or billeted in hovel-like accommodation, often miles from towns and terribly isolated. The uniform seems to have given cause for complaint with the greatcoats in particular being described as "suitable only for maternity wear". Humiliatingly, Land Girls were not admitted into canteens shared by the WRNS,

ATS and WAAF until August 1942; even then, they were often forbidden to buy chocolates and cigarettes reserved for the Forces. Kindly Servicemen and women would regularly buy tea and food for the Girls and bring it outside to them.

Joyce Trueman was a Land Girl based in the WLA hostel on Lodgefield Lane, Hoveringham, during the war. She had been born in London and five members of her immediate family had been killed in the Blitz. The Hoveringham hostel had been a private residence, but was taken over by the War Ag in 1942. It housed twelve Girls, who were under the care of a female Warden. The Girls slept on straw mattresses in three bedrooms and there was always a hot meal at the hostel in the evening. When Joyce was stationed there in 1943, a rota ensured two Girls did the washing up each evening. This was a particularly unpopular chore as it meant missing a dance at the Elm Tree, three hundred yards away and packed with personnel from RAF Syerston. (By 1945, when Margaret Rigley, also a Land Girl, was based at Hoveringham, the warden conveniently had two sisters who "kept house" and the Girls were spared the dreaded washing up duties.)

Other hostels were at Calverton, Hockerton (described as a ghastly wooden "chicken shed"), Hawksworth, Farndon and Collingham, to name but a few. Collingham had a purpose-built hostel and was considered the height of luxury by the Girls billeted there.

Margaret Rigley has mixed memories of RAF Syerston, ranging from going to dances at the Officers' Mess to walking the hedges bordering the airfield with a local farm hand, looking for rat holes. The poison was fed down the hole via a spoon tied with string to the end of a bamboo cane. On one occasion, whilst working in a field at the end of the main runway at Syerston, Margaret straightened up to watch a heavy bomber on its final approach; she was alarmed to see that the aircraft appeared to be aiming directly at her and the other Girls. The bomber's enormous wheels grew closer until the Girls, by now terrified, flung themselves face down in the field. The brief glimpse Margaret got of the pilot laughing as he passed overhead remains with her.

The local Land Girls were transported to the farms and airfields in what was known as the "buggy" (a jeep). At RAF Newton, three miles from Hoveringham, one Land Girl was being taught how to drive the buggy for the first time, the grass runway making an ideal practice ground (Health and Safety regulations would not feature for another sixty years!). All went well until a bomber unexpectedly appeared low out of the clouds and proceeded to land. The instructor presumably saw it because the buggy violently accelerated and veered off the runway to safety, the driving lesson ending somewhat abruptly. The pilot's opinion of what he encountered is unrecorded.

In 1943, Joyce Trueman was potato-riddling in a field close to Hoveringham and paused to watch a Lancaster pass overhead in the direction of nearby RAF Syerston. To her horror, its port wing sheared off and the aircraft plunged into the steep wooded slope just across the River Trent where it exploded. Afterwards, a red "scar" was visible where the rock had been exposed by the impact and it was many years before the trees grew back to conceal the spot where seven men had died in an instant. The disfigured area of hillside is well-remembered in the village.

By July 1943, the Land Army was at its peak strength of over 87,000. The Government suspended recruitment as women were required urgently in aircraft factories and munitions industries.

As a result, farmers were increasingly assisted by POWs, many of them Italian and German.

The use of Prisoners of War was first mooted in 1940 but it was not until July 1941 that the first Italian POWs appeared, 2,400 of them arriving in time to help with the harvest with a further 28,000 expected to be put to work before long. The POWs lived in camps initially and were escorted in gangs by armed soldiers to the farms, but from January 1942 "good conduct" prisoners were allowed to reside permanently on the farms.

Farmers applied to the local War Ag for a prisoner – just as they had to for Land Girls – and they also had to pay the War Ag for each prisoner: they were not free labour. In accordance with the Geneva Convention, each prisoner received six pence to a shilling a day and the demand for Italians POWs was immediate and considerable – male muscles being preferable to Land Girls, especially where heavy work was involved such as ditching or beet-lifting. There was resentment from regular farm workers and Land Girls who watched the POWs arriving each day with ample army rations and equipped with rubber boots and capes. In addition, the prisoners worked fewer hours than other workers.

Words such as "idle" and "work-shy" crop up – perhaps unfairly – when Italian POWs are remembered by local farmers. Other descriptions include "excitable" or "born lazy". Another local farmer had little time for Italian soldiers in general, commenting: "well, they were very quick to put their hands up, weren't they?". Some prisoners suffered verbal abuse and taunts as they were carted around in the lorries; others struck up friendships on the farms and were popular with the farmers' families because they were good with young children. Freda Klingbeil lived on a farm at Syerston during the war and spoke a little Italian; she taught the POWs English as they worked together in the fields. (She later married a German POW and they lived in Flintham for the next three decades.)

Farms in Hoveringham and Gonalston employed Italian POWs from a camp at nearby Woodborough. Norman Clarke was a young boy at Ferry Farm in Hoveringham in the war and used to watch the Italians cooking their meals. By means of some culinary alchemy, the foreigners conjured up spaghetti from dried egg.

Italian POWs worked at Kneeton, the farm adjacent to RAF Syerston's south-western boundary. These men planted young trees, amongst their many tasks, and the testament to their labour, are some of the mature woods visible today on the skyline above Hoveringham. The Italians were delivered daily in a truck from Allington, a large POW camp a few miles south of Newark. Later in the war, some prisoners lived in the top floor of a very humble barn opposite Kneeton church and slept on straw palliasses. The entire contingent of prisoners disappeared one day: only when a lorry of soldiers was despatched from Langar to search for them was it discovered that, far from making a break for freedom, the Italians had gone no further than local cottages in search of company.

By July 1943, more than 37,000 POWs were working on the land with a further 36,000 requested by the Minister of Agriculture to help with the 1944 harvest. German POWs made their first appearance on the land in 1944, for the potato harvest. Unlike the Italians, they were not allowed to live on the farms and they were not put to work alongside the Italians in case of "trouble". Germans appear to have been regarded as more conscientious workers, one farmer commenting that "one German is worth three Italians".

Chris Lee, who grew up on a farm at East Stoke, a village two miles north east of RAF Syerston, recalls three German POWs being assigned to their farm. Emil, Conrad and Ernst were brought daily on a bus from Allington, and worked diligently from 8am until 5pm. However, when the Nuremburg trials commenced after the war, Ernst refused to work and this protest resulted in all three men being sent back to their camp in disgrace for the day. (Although the trials were held after the war had ended, many POWs were not repatriated to their own countries for some time, in some cases not until the end of 1948.) In 1946, a fifth of all farm work in Britain was still being done by German POWs.

Everyday life in Britain changed beyond all recognition to adapt to the deprivations and fears created by the war. But if there was one aspect of the conflict above all others which was visible daily to villagers in Hoveringham and the Trent valley, it was the war taking place above them, in the skies. German planes brought terrible destruction to Nottingham, Newark and surrounding villages. The Government's response to this onslaught was the construction of gigantic airfields on an unprecedented scale, resulting in huge numbers of RAF bombers flying day and night over this hitherto quiet, rural area. The war in the air over Nottinghamshire is clearly remembered by those people who witnessed it, more than six decades after the heavy bombers fell silent for the last time.

Chapter Three

"SOWING THE WIND..."

Bombing from the air was first tried in 1911 by Italian pilots against a Turkish camp in Libya. By the simple action of extending an arm out of the aircraft and letting go of a bomb (in fact it was a grenade), it was found that a degree of control could be exerted over the surprised unfortunates on the ground below.

Britain's first foray into strategic bombing was in October 1914, when the Royal Naval Air Service (RNAS) attacked Zeppelin factories. Her first experience of being on the receiving end of aerial bombing came on 19 January 1915, when a Zeppelin dropped bombs on sleepy Sheringham in Norfolk. The incident is commemorated by a plaque in the town.

London was bombed by Zeppelins in June 1915, with the loss of five lives. By the end of the First World War, over 1,400 deaths (mostly civilians) had been recorded as a result of aerial attacks. Only primitive warnings existed to alert the population to these raids, in the form of policemen wearing placards and blowing whistles. During the course of the war, about forty Zeppelins were shot down by pilots. Zeppelins could fly great distances without refuelling and, between 1915 and 1918, over a dozen Zeppelins flew over the River Trent in the vicinity of Hoveringham, as Nottingham was one of their targets. In time, the twin-engined German Gotha aircraft appeared. These were long-range daylight bombers, and seventeen Gotha attacks on London were recorded during the First World War.

The shock to the British people was enormous: their island fortress, protected by water for so long, was suddenly at the mercy of enemy assaults from the air. Far from causing mass panic and mayhem, which had been Germany's intention, British anger grew at this new tactic. It was not all one-sided, either: Britain dropped over 500 tons of bombs on Germany in 1918 under the authority of Brigadier General Sir Hugh Trenchard, who was to become the Chief of Air Staff after the war. His aim was to target centres of war material production and to hit the morale of the "working classes" employed in them and living nearby. In 1918, Trenchard (nicknamed "Boom" because of his loud voice) oversaw the formation of the Royal Air Force from what had been the Royal Flying Corps and the Royal Naval Air Service. The fledgling Air Force enjoyed total independence from the Army and Navy, but unfortunately received scant financial investment.

Domination of the skies, and in particular the bombardment of enemy targets and morale, was strongly advocated by Trenchard and his colleagues such as Charles Portal and Arthur Harris who had served with him in squadrons in the twenties. Like him, they had seen the effectiveness of bombing campaigns and were vigorous supporters of this strategy, pushing for the expansion of bomber squadrons. These senior RAF officers were convinced that bombing could reduce the need for land battles like the horrific ones they had seen in the First World War, and these men were destined to have crucial roles in defining Bomber Command's role in the Second World War.

In 1940, control of the skies over England was vital to the success of Germany's planned invasion of Britain, codenamed Operation "Sealion". Although the British Army was only just getting up from its knees after Dunkirk and the newly-formed Home Guard had few armaments with which to repel an invasion, Hitler was fully aware of the giant challenge he faced in crossing the Channel: Britain was well defended ashore and moreover enjoyed the protection of the powerful Royal Navy. Hitler was not confident when it came to naval warfare (he allegedly did not set eyes on the sea until he was over forty) and travelled from Paris one sunny day to gaze across at the white cliffs of Dover. By coincidence, Napoleon had done exactly the same over a century before when planning his invasion of Britain. Both men were ultimately forced to abandon their plans to invade Britain and both then turned their sights east instead – towards Russia.

To achieve the necessary aerial domination, Hitler issued an order on 16 July that the British Air Force was to be "eliminated". Reichsmarschall Goering, the head of the Luftwaffe, had confidently assured Hitler that the RAF was strong but would break under the weight of the Luftwaffe's attack. Yet he underestimated the number of operational aircraft available to the RAF by such a catastrophic margin that Sealion was destined never to even get more than its feet wet.

The Battle of Britain began on 10 July when Sealion raised its head and the Luftwaffe mounted its first attacks, particularly against British shipping in the Channel and the Channel naval ports. On 8 August nearly 1,500 sorties were carried out by the

Luftwaffe across a 500 mile front, attacking a variety of targets. Hurricanes and Spitfires at fighter stations along the south and east coast of Britain were constantly scrambled to intercept the invaders. Initially, Hurricane squadrons outnumbered Spitfires by a two to one margin. The Spitfire was the faster plane, but the Hurricane had a smaller turning radius which provided critical greater manoeuvrability in a dog-fight.

Britain enjoyed a crucial advantage: she had a sophisticated network of radar and other early warning means, unparalleled anywhere in the world. The Royal Observer Corps also played a vital part in ensuring very few German bombers entered British airspace undetected. Germany developed her radar systems to become equally effective, particularly the Freya radar (although its range was limited to 100 miles and it was not accurate at determining aircraft altitude), but in the summer of 1940, the RAF held the aces where early warning was concerned. As one RAF fighter pilot commented, these defences ensured that they wasted "no petrol, no energy, no time…" in locating the enemy bombers.

Adolf Galland, the fighter ace and head of the Luftwaffe Fighter Arm, noted the German pilots' information was at best three hours old, whereas, with the advantage of radar information, RAF pilots were warned in mere minutes. The German bombers would be picked up by radar as they crossed the Pas de Calais, a full 25 minutes' flying time away, giving the RAF fighters sufficient time to scramble and climb to 20,000 feet to ambush them. Wave after wave of German bombers crossed the English coastline. Goering's air crews encountered a strong and determined fighter presence.

Goering altered his strategy to concentrate on obliterating RAF fighter bases, beginning on 13 August (Adler Tag, or "Eagle

Day"). Some 700 sorties were flown by Fighter Command that day and Churchill who was inspecting coastal defences, stopped what he was doing to watch the fighting far above him. Fourteen RAF fighters were lost compared to 46 German bombers.

The Battle of Britain was at its peak in August 1940 and was fought over the south-eastern counties of England. "Hellfire Corner", the area of Kent nearest France, and incorporating Dover, Folkestone and Lympne, witnessed more fatalities on both sides than anywhere else in England during the whole of the rest of the Battle. The sound of aircraft machine guns could be heard clearly by farm workers harvesting in the fields below; if a German aircraft was shot down, a deafening cheer would go up from the spectators. The Land Girls requested tin helmets in the most dangerous areas, as a protection against falling shrapnel, and more than one girl took cover under her tractor after being fired at by German gunners. Some of the girls wore the helmets on their bottoms as they decided this was their most vulnerable area whilst they worked bending over!

The summer of 1940 was a glorious one and the stubble of the harvested fields took on a rich yellow hue as if warm honey had been poured over the landscape. Far above, though, the deadly airborne battles left hundreds of vapour trails which meandered deceptively lazily across the blue skies. The contrast between bucolic beauty and absolute carnage could not have been greater. Up in the air, for fighter pilots sitting behind fuel tanks containing eighty-five gallons of high octane fuel, fire was understandably a primary fear. If the fuel ignited, it could reach catastrophically high temperatures within moments. Pilots reckoned that the most time they had to get out of the cockpit was eight seconds; if you took ten, you were not going to survive. Wrestling to slide the canopy back at speeds of over 180 mph was also no easy matter when the air pressure was trying to push the canopy forwards. Ditching in the Channel was no better: the heavy engine weight, frequently meant that the aircraft nosedived for the seabed immediately on contact with the water. Those pilots who baled out into the Channel had around four hours before hypothermia set in, assuming both that their injuries did not kill them before and that they had managed to inflate their lifejackets. Merchant seamen, remembering their treatment at the hands of the Luftwaffe at Dunkirk, were occasionally hostile to floating pilots; RAF pilots discovered that the quickest way to confirm their friendly nationality to the seamen was to swear at them in unmistakably English terms.

Mounting losses of trained fighter pilots due to fatigue amongst both pilots and ground crews was becoming a major problem for the RAF. The ground crews could have an aircraft patched up, re-armed, re-fuelled and ready to take off again in fifteen minutes. At the height of the Battle, the turn-around could be as little as four minutes. Some pilots were flying up to four sorties a day and were so exhausted, they were seen to fall asleep as they ate in the mess halls. The Civilian Repair Organisation worked 12 hour shifts and helped get damaged aircraft back into the air, but with so many fighter bases out of action from the relentless enemy attacks – including even the talismanic Biggin Hill – things were beginning to look bleak for Fighter Command and the nation.

Had Hitler adhered to his original strategy of targeting airfields, aircraft and aircraft manufacturing industries, the outcome of the Battle of Britain might well have been entirely different. However, events intervened on 24 August, when a Heinkel He-111, which may have been lost, unintentionally and against Hitler's express orders, dropped its bombs on the City of London. In that moment, the Heinkel crew (who were subsequently punished by Goering and transferred to an infantry unit) unwittingly ensured that the bombing war was to change forever. Until that point, both sides had ensured that civilians were not targeted by their bombers. Hitler had expressly forbidden that bombs be released above London, apart from over the docks.

Retaliation was immediate. Desperate to boost morale at home, Churchill ordered that Berlin be attacked. Despite Bomber Command's pleas for more time to prepare for such a major raid, the order stood, and the German capital was attacked on 25, 28 and 29 August. Just as Churchill had gambled, Hitler, who had promised the Germans that their cities were beyond the reach of the RAF, swore that British cities would be "eradicated" in revenge. The Luftwaffe was commanded to switch its offensive from airfields and other strategic targets to the British capital. The Blitz began in earnest on 7 September with a huge raid on London's docks: the gloves were well and truly off.

Hitler's abrupt change of plan was a major factor in the failure of Operation Sealion. By switching its attention to London and other British cities, the Luftwaffe gave the RAF fighter squadrons precious time to repair, to regroup and – critically – to rest their exhausted pilots.

Bomber Command, meanwhile, had been employed in low-level attacks, pounding Hitler's invasion barges and fleets as they waited in various Channel ports for the order to cross the Channel. Guy Gibson (later of Dambusters fame) who participated in these raids, aptly christened this onslaught "The Battle of the Barges". Blenheims, Hampdens and Wellingtons were employed by the Command for these forays. Each squadron was given a particular port to target – Boulogne, Calais, Dunkirk, Ostend and Antwerp were amongst the main ones – and then individual crews were told to focus on a specific basin. Each basin could contain anywhere from 200 to 400 barges and the attacking crews could clearly see that these were heavily laden with tanks and guns. Hitler planned to send over 150,000 invasion troops across to Britain. Many of these troops were billeted in the warehouses by the barges and suffered heavy casualties in the bombardment. Bomber Command's aircrews played a vital role in thwarting the invasion, which is often overlooked. Between June 1940 and the end of that year, nearly 330 aircraft from the Command were lost and 1,400 aircrew killed, missing or taken prisoner. It is the heroism of Fighter Command – "The Few" – that tends to be remembered: their heart-stopping battles were, after all, played out largely above the British countryside and in full view of a sizeable "home crowd".

The Battle of Britain was over by the end of October 1940 and Germany's plans to invade Britain were in tatters; the Luftwaffe had suffered dreadful losses at the hands of the RAF fighters through its policy of daytime raids, and had failed to secure the skies for Hitler. The approaching winter weather rendered the Channel uncrossable by Hitler's invasion craft and flat-bottomed barges, and the mighty Royal Navy continued to be a major deterrent. Sealion had been slain.

The Blitz, however, was anything but over. Since the end of September 1940, the Luftwaffe had altered its tactics to bomb by night in order to avoid the RAF fighters, which could not operate in the dark. During one such night-time attack on London in December 1940, Air Vice-Marshal Arthur Harris went up onto the roof of the Air Ministry to observe the raid. St Paul's Cathedral was "standing out in the midst of an ocean of fire", he wrote in his memoirs. Such was the sight that he asked Air Chief Marshal Portal, to join him and witness the city's devastation. Harris, who knew full well that the heavy bombers being designed for the RAF would be capable, in the future, of delivering colossal bomb loads to German cities, said to Portal: "They are sowing the wind, and now they will reap the whirlwind". The phrase was from the Old Testament. It was later repeated by both Harris (to aircrews) and Churchill (to the Canadian Parliament) and is remembered as one of the most famous – and prophetic – statements of the war.

Struggling to come to terms with more than 40,000 civilians fatalities in the Blitz and with their backs to the wall, the British yearned to avenge their dead and to hurt the enemy in its own homeland; many Londoners said they could take the German bombs as long as they knew "Jerry was getting the same" – and more – from the RAF. Concerns about descending to the level of the enemy – in terms of the morality of bombing civilians – were voiced by many at this point, and, indeed, grew as the RAF bombing campaign intensified over the years; but in 1940, support for striking back and taking the war to Germany was widespread amongst the population.

Fighter Command had defended Britain heroically, but Bomber Command's hour was coming.

Chapter Four

THE BOMBER OFFENSIVE

"Hitler built a fortress around Europe, but he forgot to put a roof on it."
Franklin D. Roosevelt

The RAF had received little investment in the 1920s, but the growing alarm at Hitler's policies in the 1930s led to an increasing amount of money being spent on aircraft production. In 1936, the RAF was divided into Bomber Command, Fighter Command, Coastal Command and Training Command. The RAF Volunteer Reserve was also created that year and many young men duly joined up, some harbouring visions of dog-fights and glory as described by First World War pilots, others because they wanted to avoid, at any cost, the horrors of trench warfare endured by their fathers.

Undoubtedly, the common bond uniting these volunteers was a love of flying. In Bomber Command, those who were not going to be pilots enrolled on courses to learn the skills of air gunners, wireless operators, bomb-aimers, navigators and, from 1942, flight engineers. Of those training to be pilots, a large proportion learned the basics of flight at the controls of sturdy Tiger Moths. In December 1939, the Empire Air Training Scheme was inaugurated to train aircrew. The scheme saw the creation of

180 flying schools in Canada, Australia, New Zealand, Southern Rhodesia and South Africa. British aircrew were sent to learn to fly abroad, alongside fellow volunteers from those countries, in a safe environment far removed from the dual hazards of British weather and enemy aircraft. About a third of all aircrew were trained overseas under this scheme. In addition, no fewer than 16,000 British aircrew were trained in America (with the loss of 200 men and ten instructors killed in training). Despite its "Neutrality Act" of 1935, with its aim of keeping the US out of other peoples' wars, America was keen to assist the Allies as much as possible. It took an average of two years to train bomber aircrew at a cost of around £10,000 per trainee – more than it then cost to educate someone at Oxford or Cambridge. Overall, 125,000 men volunteered to join Bomber Command as aircrew during the course of the war. Nearly half of them would not live to see the end of it.

At the outbreak of war, Bomber Command consisted of 53 squadrons, 33 of which were fully operational. Of those, ten had been despatched to France to support the British Expeditionary Force. The 488 bombers available – Blenheims, Hampdens, Whitleys, Wellingtons and Fairey Battles – were all twin-or single-engined, all at least six years old in terms of design, and none of them were capable of carrying truly heavy bomb loads. Some, such as the Wellington (also known affectionately as the "Wimpy" or "Flying Cigar") were regarded as doughty workhorses, capable of withstanding a great deal of damage whilst remaining airborne, whereas others were seen as little more than death-traps. The Hampden could carry a useful bomb load of 4,000lb, but was so cramped that some crews, wedged inside, nicknamed it the "Flying Suitcase". It had a lethal blind spot and also became known, ominously, as the "Flying Coffin". Other pilots said it was an excellent aircraft as long as the narrow fuselage – which was barely three feet wide towards the tail – was taken into account and less rudder was used when turning, to prevent it "skidding" across the sky. There was definitely a knack to flying it. In the winter of 1939–40, Bomber Command carried out daylight "armed reconnaissance sorties" with these outdated and lightly-defended aircraft, and suffered disastrous losses.

In October 1940 Air Marshal Sir Charles Portal left Bomber Command to become Chief of the Air Staff, and Sir Richard Pierse replaced him. Portal directed Pierse to carry out large-scale attacks on major industrial centres, regardless of the fact that they were frequently sited in urban areas. "Material destruction" was Portal's primary aim, followed by "hardship and dislocation", hopefully causing a logistical headache for the Nazis who would have to relocate thousands of homeless workers. The expectation was that industry would grind to a halt as workers were disrupted and demoralised. The Command had around 500 aircraft but was still awaiting precisely the right weapons to implement its full might in the way that Portal envisaged. The massive raids that were to feature in the coming years were an aspiration.

Bomber Command's impact on the enemy was limited by its aircraft's flying range and payload. The crews were also hindered by a lack of navigational aids and crude bomb-aiming sights. Many young men died having done no more than make potholes in German fields. In 1940, a report shocked Bomber Command by confirming that only one in five bombers was dropping its bombs within five miles of its target. Unsustainable numbers of aircraft were being lost to German fighters during these daylight raids; consequently, the

Command switched to the cover of night bombing, despite barely half the aircraft being suitable for night operations and the crews having little or no experience of this new practice. The dreadful toll on men and aircraft was reduced but so was bombing accuracy.

Coventry was attacked in November 1940. With great efficiency, the German bombers criss-crossed the city, which was reduced to a smouldering ruin overnight. Over 500 civilians were killed and the British nation was horrified. As a reprisal, Mannheim was bombed the following month by a force of 134 Bomber Command aircraft: the largest raid by the Command to date, and their first purely urban attack. Wellingtons dropped incendiaries, the glare from the ensuing flames illuminating the target for the following bombers. The stakes in the bombing campaign were being raised inexorably as the tit-for-tat raids grew in intensity.

The Germans had, by now, woken up to the damage that Bomber Command was becoming capable of inflicting. The following year, 1941, German night fighters began to be a menace, as German radar systems, and their pilots' tactics, became increasingly sophisticated to counter the threat from Bomber Command.

British and German civilians alike were experiencing the same horrors as the bombing campaigns were stepped up. The spirited defiance shown by Londoners during the Blitz – as well as the residents of other British cities in subsequent bombing raids – was also evident in German cities. If breaking morale had been a primary objective of bombing campaigns on both sides, it was to be proved ultimately unsuccessful.

Sheffield was one of the English cities to be bombed, and the glow as it burned was clearly visible from Newark. Nottingham was bombed on several occasions, and local people clearly remember the sound of the German bombers and the frantic firing of anti-aircraft guns defending the city. Following one attack on 8 May 1941, some parts of the city had no water, gas or electricity for three days. Ten days later, whilst the funerals of those killed in the raid were being conducted, a lone German bomber flew over another part of the city and machine-gunned the streets.

On 14 November 1940, a reconnaissance aircraft – probably a Junkers 88 (with a crew of four or five) – was engaged by anti-aircraft fire as it took photographs over Nottingham, forcing it to alter course back towards the River Trent. It was followed by an RAF fighter which chased it along the Trent valley: the pursuit was witnessed by many people in the Hoveringham area as the intruder fled in the direction of the North Sea. (This may have been the German aircraft seen by a resident of Thurgarton, near Hoveringham, who heard machine guns from a plane flying low above him as he crossed a field to fetch his newspaper from Thurgarton station. It was not a pleasant experience as he was particularly exposed in the open.)

Newark, a few miles further downstream on the River Trent, was bombed eight times during the war, including six times in the first months of 1941. The most destructive attack was on 7 March 1941 when Ransome & Marles' factory which made ball bearings for gun turrets was bombed twice in one day with the loss of forty lives. The German pilots had simply followed the main London to Edinburgh railway line all the way to the factory, which was located only a few hundred yards from Newark station. The noise of German bombers was distinct from any other type of aircraft: "a throbbing hum". One employee at RAF Syerston likened the sound of their engines to someone murmuring, "I'm coming, I'm coming, I'm coming".

On occasion, incendiary bombs fell in the villages on the approach to Nottingham and are well remembered by locals who, as children, retrieved them from fields (and, once, from a greenhouse) before dismantling them out of curiosity. The children at Hoveringham School were visited by the local policeman who reminded them not to touch bombs of any kind, following an incident when a child had brought an incendiary home and his mother had innocently placed it on the mantelpiece. One of the teenage residents of the Borstal prison in Lowdham picked up an incendiary and put it in his coat; it was swiftly hurled into a ditch when his friends noticed smoke coming from his pocket.

Despite bad winter weather at the beginning of 1941, operations continued. There were persistent demands from the Admiralty which wanted the RAF bombers to target the shipyards that made U-boats – for so long the dread of British merchant convoys and the Navy. Over 30,000 merchant seamen died during the war as a result of attacks by U-boats and German battleships. Coastal Command was already employed defending these convoys, being equipped with aircraft capable of flying for long distances over water, such as Sunderland flying boats. (The Sunderland could rescue sailors from the water and was nicknamed "the Porcupine" by German pilots because it bristled with guns and could defend itself vigorously.) Ship-building yards and harbours therefore continued to be prime objectives for Bomber Command: in the early summer, Hamburg, Kiel and Bremen were hit repeatedly by attacking forces of more than 100 bombers, although the raid on Bremen resulted in the then highest number of bombers shot down by German night fighters. Hamburg, where a third of all U-boats were constructed, also sheltered enormous battleships such as the

Hoveringham from Kneeton village, 2009. (The Old Elm Tree pub in foreground). Photo: author.

The same view of Hoveringham, early twentieth century. Aircraft used the three poplar trees in the centre of the photo to line up with the runway at RAF Syerston.

A stricken Stuka plunges earthwards to its destruction during the Battle of Britain, 18 August 1940, West Broyle near Chichester. Photo: WW2 Images.

Poignant messages from German visitors as war looms, Kneeton Guest House, 1939. Courtesy: Jack Barnet.

WAAFs battling with a barrage balloon. Photo: PRO.

The Fire Crew, based at Lowdham, who attended both Lancaster crashes in Hoveringham, which many of the crew found particularly distressing. Mr. Morley (inset) of Morley's Garage, Lowdham, was the crew Captain. Photo: Mary Hall (nee Morley).

The Hoveringham and Thurgarton Home Guard Unit. Photo: S. Crowder.

The concrete remains of the Royal Observer Corps
lookout post, Lowdham, which had uninterrupted views
across the Trent Valley. RAF Syerston's giant hangars
are visible on the far horizon.

The Land Girls' hostel in Hoveringham. Lancaster JB125 flew very low over its roof moments before striking the ground in the fields in front of the hostel. Photo: Joyce Truman.

Land Girls at the hostel on Lodgefield Lane, Hoveringham, c. 1943. Photo: Joyce Truman.

Land Girls on parade in Nottingham (wearing their "whistling cords"!). Photo: Joyce Truman.

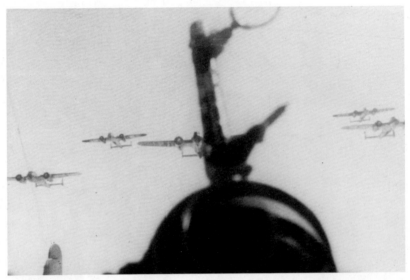

On their way to London.... Dornier 17s during the Battle of Britain, photographed by a Dornier rear-gunner. Photo: WW2 Images.

An RAF reconnaissance photograph of massed German invasion barges in Boulogne, waiting to take part in Operation "Sealion". Photo: PRO.

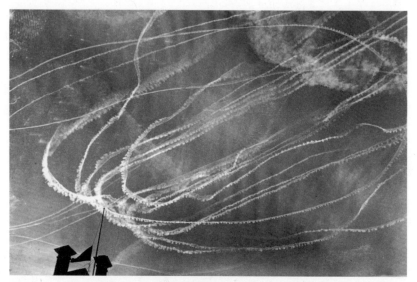

Vapour trails, lazily drifting across the summer sky over London during the Battle of Britain. Photo: WW2 Images.

A Me 109, shot down during the Battle of Britain, being investigated by a herd of inquisitive sheep. Photo: WW2 Images.

A truly formidable weapon of war.... the Lancaster. Photo: author.

Sir Arthur Harris, Commander in
Chief, Bomber Command.
Photo: WW2 Images.

The cockpit. There was an armour-plated panel directly behind the pilot's head, although this offered scant protection from a German 20mm shell. The flight engineer's seat, to the right of the pilot's, is folded away in its stowed position, to allow access to the bomb-aimer's position in the nose.

Looking aft down the austere fuselage to the rear-gunner's turret, the loneliest place in the plane.

RAF Bombers over St. Vith in the Ardennes, December 1944, assisting ground forces to repel a last-minute charge by the Germans.
Photo: PRO.

Trainee bomber
crews under
instruction.
Photo: WW2 Images.

Not just training crews came to grief on routine flights. The crew of
Lancaster PD368 (No. 9 Squadron) stand, with expressions ranging from
sheepish to relieved, beside what remains of their aircraft, after it
lost power on take off from Bardney in Lincolnshire, on New Year's Day
1945. The aircraft veered off the runway, struck an earth mound and was
launched briefly into the air, before belly-flopping into the trees. The
aircraft which took off just before them also crashed, sadly with the loss
of its crew. Photo: WW2 Images.

Lancaster MkIII JA893 which did not return to Syerston in September 1943. The crew ditched after being shot down by a German fighter. The bomb aimer was killed in the attack and the rear gunner died of injuries in the dinghy. The five surviving crew were rescued, but were subsequently killed a month later, on a raid on Hanover. Photo: PRO.

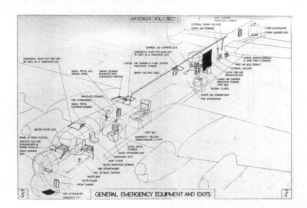

The completion of their training: crews at No. 5 LFS, before being posted to operational squadrons. Photo: Picture the Past.

No room for error: the view from the very end of the main runway, RAF Syerston, 2009. The sailing lakes are visible; the River Trent is closer than the lakes, but out of sight below the fields. Photo: author.

RAF Syerston in April 1944. Photo: Milan Petrovic.

An air raid shelter at Syerston, with the standby set building behind, 2009. Photo: author.

Rather a bleak place to work! The standby set building, RAF Syerston, 2009. Photo: author.

Remnants of the war: the giant J-type hangars and the control tower,
RAF Syerston, 2009. Photo: author.

The perimeter track at Syerston, 2009. Photo: author.

Boat Lane (also called Ferry Lane), Hoveringham, as it appeared during the war. Kneeton village is on the hilltop beyond. The Lancasters lined up with the main runway at RAF Syerston by flying over the poplar trees in the centre of the photo.
Photo: Nancy Tooley.

The Old Elm Tree pub, Hoveringham, during the war.
Photo: Eileen Lawton.

The riverbank at the Old Elm Tree pub, Hoveringham, during the war.
Photo: Nancy Tooley.

Gypsy Lane, leading steeply up to Kneeton church, December 2009.
Photo: author.

Sgt. Lawrence McElroy of
the RCAF scratched his name
on the wall at Manor Farm,
Hoveringham in 1944. A few
months later, he was shot down
and badly injured. He spent the
rest of the war as a POW and
died in the 1970s.

Lancasters from 106 Squadron at dispersal, RAF Syerston, 1943.
Photo: Flypast Magazine.

106 Squadron at Syerston, winter 1942–43. Guy Gibson is standing with his
back to the camera, hands on hips. Photo: Goulding-Garbett Collection.

Nigger's name tag, with Gibson's name and squadron number engraved on it. Nigger (Guy Gibson's black labrador), was run over and killed on the day of the Dams Raid and his name was chosen by Gibson as the call-sign to indicate whether the Mohne Dam had been breached (it was). Nigger's grave is at RAF Scampton. Photo: Author.

Wng Cmdr Guy Gibson (CO 106 Squadron), flanked by (left) Squadron Leader Searby and (right) Squadron Leader Ward-Hunt, RAF Syerston, March 1943. Gibson's Lancaster, Admiral Prune, is behind.

Another Lancaster destined not to return to Syerston: this one was from 106 Squadron, which crashed at Blida, North Africa whilst on a "Shuttle Raid" in 1943. Photo: PRO.

45,000 ton Tirpitz. Wilhelmshaven, another port which cradled the fearsome Bismarck, was a similar target. The Bismarck was sunk in 1941, but the Tirpitz proved to be more elusive.

In May 1941, the Germans entered Greece and Yugoslavia, although this incursion was to be totally eclipsed by Hitler's decision the following month to invade the Soviet Union.

Stirlings, Manchesters and Halifaxes were now participating in Bomber Command's night bombing raids in increasing numbers, joining the Wellingtons, Whitleys and Hampdens. High Capacity (HC) bombs weighing 4,000lbs were dropped by Wellingtons for the first time at the end of March 1942, dramatically increasing the Command's ability to inflict serious damage on the enemy. (In time the heaviest standard bomb was 12,000lb, although, even these were to be dwarfed by the RAF's mammoth 22,000lb "Tallboy" bombs.) By the end of 1941, Bomber Command had 58 squadrons, 23 of which were flying Wellingtons.

Events took a decisive turn globally on a sleepy Sunday morning on 13 December when the Japanese bombed the American fleet in Pearl Harbour. By goading America, the "Sleeping Giant", into joining forces with the Allies, Japan ensured that the conflict escalated instantly into global war.

In 1941, Churchill had stated that the one thing that would bring Hitler down was an "absolutely devastating attack by very heavy bombers" on the German homeland. Consequently, in February 1942, Bomber Command was issued a new directive: to hit "enemy morale" by the use of "area bombing", depriving German workers (and inevitably civilians) of their homes and causing terror. Incendiary bombs were used extensively as these were particularly successful at destroying towns.

In March that year, the Command received a new chief, Air Marshal Arthur Harris, known as "Butch" by aircrews, "Butcher" by his critics and, most famously, "Bomber" Harris by the British public. Harris possessed a single-minded determination to see a job through, combined with an iron-clad conviction that bombing cities could win the war from the skies and save many Allied soldiers' lives by obviating the need for land battles. At the same time, he was opposed to his bomber crews being used as an accessory to the Army, saying that the Command was unsuited to that role (yet after D-Day, the Command proved it could bomb with great precision to assist the troops on the ground). He was vehement about the merits of a sustained bombing campaign, and he was certainly not squeamish about inflicting its associated casualties on German civilians.

He is remembered as a tough individual. Such was the high regard in which he was held by his crews, that one former Flight Engineer stated: "We would have flown through a hurricane for him if he'd asked us to". He could be scathing, and when his deputy, Air Vice Marshal Saundby, suggested an alternative method of locating enemy targets, Harris returned Saundby's note with a curt "Try ferrets" scrawled across it.

With only 600 aircraft (fourteen squadrons of which comprised four-engined bombers) at his disposal when he took over, Harris immediately began to overhaul Bomber Command in the teeth of opposition from the War Office and Admiralty, clamouring over the same scarce resources, which bombers consumed in prodigious quantities. He was also confronted with the dismal fact that approximately 2,000 valuable Bomber Command aircrew had already been incarcerated as POWs on the Continent. (This figure would rise to 10,000 by the end of the war.)

Persistent demands from the Admiralty in 1942 resulted in Harris reluctantly relinquishing some of his precious bombers to attack the battleship Tirpitz, which escaped – for the time being, at least – with minor damage. German ports in the north-west of the country continued to receive Bomber Command's attention and these were starting to show signs of repeated drubbings, although the U-boat pens proved hard to penetrate. These were protected by reinforced concrete roofs up to twelve feet thick, but the Command's bombs did manage to wreak immense havoc on surrounding maintenance and communications sites.

March 1942 saw the ancient and beautiful Baltic port of Lubeck disappear in flames after a Bomber Command raid. The attack was justified by the Command because an aircraft factory was based there. It was also used by the Germans for importing iron ore from Sweden, and was a vital supply link to German troops in Russia. Crucially, however, the city was wooden and thus presented a golden opportunity for Harris to see the effectiveness of incendiary bombs. Such was the devastation that the RAF crews coined the phrase "to Lubeck" a target – meaning to pulverise it. 1,000 people were killed. (Rostock, another Baltic wooden city, suffered an identical fate a month later.) The Germans were outraged at the destruction of such a cultural gem, and retaliatory raids were not long in coming. The Luftwaffe deliberately selected English cities renowned for their history and beauty: Bath, Norwich, Exeter, York and Canterbury were all bombed in turn.

Despite some successes, Bomber Command's failure to hit its targets with consistent accuracy resulted in it being threatened with disbandment and dispersal between Coastal Command, the Army and the Navy. Harris, desperate to prove his theory that sustained bombing could succeed, saw that something had to be done urgently to convince his critics Bomber Command was capable of hurting the enemy.

Consequently, in May 1942, Harris mounted the Command's most prestigious and audacious attack to date, when over 1,000 aircraft attacked the ancient city of Cologne, the third largest city in the Reich. Everything and everybody, even crews still in training and their instructors, were roped into "Operation Millennium", which Harris freely admits in his memoirs was not only a gamble, but the worst decision he had to make in the entire war. The future of Bomber Command depended wholly on the success of the operation.

Of the 1,047 bombers that were involved, nearly 900 aircraft actually attacked their target, equating to one bomber every six seconds over the city. 600 of the bombers were Wellingtons. The bomber "stream", or flow of aircraft heading for the target, was so enormous it stretched seventy miles in total. The crews had been instructed to follow the Rhine to their target, and those crews in the aircraft at the tail end of the stream could see their objective already ablaze far ahead, like a "giant forest fire" according to one airman.

Six hundred acres of Cologne were destroyed and 469 people were killed (a relatively low number due to very good air raid warnings and shelters in the city). Thirty-nine aircraft were lost, far fewer than the 10% loss rate for which Bomber Command had braced itself. Churchill was elated and the Command's critics were silenced. Harris was knighted eleven days later.

Essen and Bremen were on the receiving end of 1,000 bomber raids in June, although they were not as severely damaged thanks to adverse weather which protected them from the bombers. These huge raids ceased thereafter, largely because of the disruption they caused to training schedules.

One of Harris's reforms was the creation of Pathfinder Squadrons in July 1942, elite squadrons whose crews, arriving first over a target, would then direct the main bombing force. The top brass at the Air Ministry was impatient to see their formation, but there was some resentment by some Squadron Commanders, who saw their finest crews "cherry-picked" from under their noses. Because only the most skilled pilots and navigators were considered for Pathfinder Squadrons, there were concerns about how this elitism would affect the morale of remaining crews. Ultimately, No 8 Group was formed to command all Pathfinder Squadrons and bombing accuracy improved markedly once the Pathfinders were implemented. The very nature of their work meant they had to circle the target, often at a dangerously low altitude, during the raid whilst monitoring and guiding the rest of the bomber stream. The Pathfinders dropped coloured flares (usually yellow or green) called target indicators, and would then radio the other aircraft to tell them which colour to aim for. A "Master Bomber", appointed before each raid, would be responsible for this task. Deputies were lined up to take over should he be shot down. It was a highly dangerous role. Franklin D. Roosevelt famously said, "Hitler built a fortress around Europe, but he forgot to put a roof on it." In fact, there was a roof, a very well-defended one, and it was costing many RAF bomber crew lives.

Sleek Mosquitos, built largely of wood and capable of 380 mph, were used increasingly by Pathfinders as the war progressed. They were unarmed in this task, relying on their speed to outrun attackers. The extreme risks to which Pathfinders were exposed, meant they were expected to fly fewer operations than other bomber crews in order to complete a tour.

Bomber Command losses were still appalling, leading Churchill, in September 1942, to order a blackout on the number of casualties. Yet despite the heavy toll on men and aircraft, with raids often flown in terrible weather, the Command was starting to land some very painful blows on the enemy.

Aircrews were also sent across the Alps to bomb Italian cities such as Genoa and Milan to persuade Italy to give up the war, the Allies having seen victory at El Alamein the previous October. These cities were lightly defended, so Italian sorties came as somewhat of a relief to bomber crews after Germany. Over 1,300 sorties were carried out to Italy in November 1942 alone, including by way of "shuttle raids". This was where bombers leaving English airfields attacked Italian targets, but instead of returning directly to their bases, they headed for the newly secured airfields in North Africa to refuel and re-arm, before proceeding to attack further targets on their way home to England.

Navigational aids were improving rapidly, and so was the Command's ability to hit targets with success. A radar installation code-named "Gee" displayed the ground to the aircraft's navigator on a grid layout and could work up to 400 miles from the home transmitter although, inevitably, it was only a matter of time before the Germans discovered its frequency and blocked it. Gee was followed by "H2S", a ground-mapping radar system introduced in

January 1943 which led to significantly more accurate navigation, utterly transforming flying for the bomber crews. "Oboe" was another new navigational device fitted, initially, to Pathfinder Mosquitos enabling their crews to attain a 75% accuracy rate when marking targets for bombers.

America had joined the strategic bombing campaign the previous summer, with precision bombing in daylight raids. Despite guns protruding from every direction and heavy armour plating, the B-17s of the US Eighth Air Force were easy prey for the German fighters until 1943 when P47 Thunderbolts and P38 Lightnings appeared and began escorting the B-17s. These fighters, however, did not have the range to reach Germany – but Mustangs (or P-51s as they were also known) certainly did: with a top speed of over 400 mph they could travel up to 600 miles from their English bases. Combined with Bomber Command's nightly raids, a relentless round-the-clock bombing onslaught was soon to be visited upon the enemy: the tide was gradually turning against the Luftwaffe.

In May 1943, "Operation Chastise", better known as the "Dambusters" raid was mounted on the Mohne, Eder and Sorpe dams in Germany. The "Bouncing Bomb" was technically an 11,000lb mine, codenamed "Upkeep". The first two dams were breached (the third was damaged) and the propaganda value to the British was inestimable; the low-level attack still inspires awe today. Thirty-four decorations were awarded to the aircrew who took part in the raid, including the Victoria Cross for Guy Gibson, who led it. The cost was high: eight of the 19 aircraft that took off from Scampton failed to return, with the loss of 55 airmen.

Like London, Cologne, Dusseldorf, Duisburg, Dortmund, Essen and other German cities in the industrial Ruhr basin were all ferociously defended. The defences did not deter Harris who repeatedly sent his bomber crews to the Ruhr. One former air gunner admitted, "I was frightened of Cologne", which was targeted in particular for its cathedral, train station and vital River Rhine bridges. With more than a hint of irony, aircrews nicknamed this region "Happy Valley".

Hamburg, with a population of one million, was always high on Bomber Command's list of targets and was attacked by 791 Bomber Command aircraft in July 1943. The petrified citizens suffered a terrible fate when a firestorm swept through the streets, the winds reaching tornado speed in places and sucking them into the core of the inferno. Others were incinerated above ground. The tremendous heat generated from the fires was bad enough, but the ferocity of the flames sucked the oxygen upwards and a great many people in shelters suffocated as a result. The heat was even felt by bomber crews in their aircraft over the city. Over 45,000 people died. After seeing the devastation, the Nazi Propaganda Minister, Joseph Goebbels announced gloomily, "We're all in the front line now".

During the summer of 1943, Bomber Command employed "Window", an invention which blinded the Wurzburg type of radar and, crucially, created a blizzard effect on the German night fighters' radar screens. Window was the simplest of devices: strips of aluminium coated in graphite, pushed in bundles out of bombers at high altitude, dispersed in the bomber's slipstream as they fell, creating false impressions on radar screens. Only the most experienced German radar operators could differentiate between falling Window and an actual bomber. Strips of Window were picked up by children in England and used as Christmas tree decorations.

As a result of Window, Bomber Command had the whip hand for a whole six weeks before the enemy overcame the problem in what was a constant battle of wits between the RAF and the Luftwaffe. Morale amongst crews was boosted monumentally. Bereft of their radar, German night fighter pilots had to revert to using their eyes and intuition to seek their prey, and to following the coloured marker flares dropped by Pathfinders, in the hope of coming across the main bomber stream. German flak-battery operators described the terror of having no radar to guide their anti-aircraft guns, which had been similarly affected by Window. "It was like being given a rifle but then being blindfolded," wrote one Hamburg defender.

Praised by Churchill in October for the Hamburg attacks, as well as successful raids on Peenemunde and Italy, Harris, seeking another opportunity to demonstrate that bombs won wars, turned his attention to Berlin. He confidently told Churchill that he planned to "wreck" Berlin and end the war.

Berlin, or "The Big City" as aircrew called it, felt the full might of Bomber Command on 18 November and again on no fewer than sixteen occasions between then and March 1944. Overall, 6,000 people were killed in the city, and one and a half million were left homeless. Far from damaging the morale of Berliners, as had happened after the first bombing raid in 1940, this Battle of Berlin stiffened their spines.

By the end of 1943, the Allies had dropped a staggering 200,000 tons of bombs on Germany.

Bad weather during the winter of 1943–44 affected operations, and heavy crew losses, especially in the first three months of 1944, caused Bomber Command's spirits to dip again. Losses in squadrons could vary capriciously from none, to half a dozen, or a constant two or three every trip. Weeks sometimes passed without a single crew in a squadron reaching the magical tally of 30 sorties to complete a tour, which would entitle them to six months' off operations, usually a brief leave period followed by some months with a training unit as an instructor.

One of the Command's worst nights occurred on 30 March 1944 when a force of nearly 800 bombers took off to attack Nuremburg. This entailed flying 400 miles over enemy-occupied territory and German homeland to reach their destination. A great many of the bombers were blown off-course northwards by unexpectedly powerful winds. Forecast cloud cover had been expected to conceal them but, in the event, the bomber crews found themselves in clear, moonlit skies at the mercy of Germany fighters. A catastrophic 95 bombers were lost. One former navigator, who was still in training at RAF Syerston, recalls sitting in the dining hall at breakfast and the room falling silent in horrified disbelief as the wireless announced the appalling news of the losses incurred by the raid.

In the spring of 1944, Bomber Command could boast 1,100 heavy bombers, some of which, despite being older models and slightly outdated – Halifaxes, Wellingtons and Short Stirlings – still proved invaluable on raids. The force was placed under the direction of the Supreme Allied Commander, Eisenhower, and April saw the implementation of the "Transportation Plan". Allied bombers specifically attempted to create a chasm in the enemy's rail network in preparation for the D-Day landings and the subsequent advance of Allied ground forces. The plan was to cut off rail supplies to Normandy whilst trying not to reveal to the enemy, in the process, where the landings were actually going to take place. For every genuine target bombed, two were hit elsewhere to mislead the Germans. Between April and June, over sixty raids took place on the French and Belgian transport system, resulting in heavy civilian casualties.

Bomber Command began to neutralise other strategic and tactical targets in France, landing hammer blows on bridges in France and German-occupied airfields. Such was the suddenness with which British aircraft, in particular those of the Tactical Air Force (TAF), could strike, that German troops removed the doors from their vehicles to facilitate a quick escape when attacked. Coastal batteries defending the beaches were pounded, and the Panzer establishment at Mailly-le-Camp, outside Paris, was bombed, although there were particularly high losses amongst the aircraft used on that raid.

The US 8th Air Force continued to mount raids by day. (The Americans had a strict policy of precision bombing and needed daylight to guarantee accuracy.) One former Bomber Command airman recalls passing waves of their aircraft taking-off for the Continent one morning, as his own bomber returned to its Lincolnshire base.

Bomber Command assisted the preparation of the ground for the Normandy landings, targeting – with great precision – airfields, ammunition dumps and military establishments. It more than rose to the challenges and countless Allied lives were arguably saved by the disruption caused by the bombers to the German network of transport and communication around the Normandy beaches prior to the invasion.

The entire south of England resembled one vast army base as tens of thousands of military personnel gathered, poised for the D-Day landings. Overnight, they vanished and fields that had been crammed with tents and soldiers lay suddenly silent, their former occupants now waiting many miles away in the gliders and landing craft that would take part in the landings. 1,200 bomber crews took part in operations on 5 and 6 June. In the weeks following D-Day, Bomber Command flew thousands of sorties in support of the troops on the ground. Its crews proved themselves highly capable of accurately targeting communication networks such as railways and tunnels.

Things were looking up for the aircrews: before April, the average time spent on an operational squadron was nine months, but, by the summer, it had shrunk to six months or even less. Although sorties were more frequent, an airman's chance of survival was increasing and this helped buoy morale. (Nearly 3,000 bombers had been lost between March 1943 and April 1944, out of nearly 75,000 sorties.)

In August 1944, the Command was released from Eisenhower's control and Harris was ordered to focus on attacking remaining war industries, in particular, synthetic oil refineries, the destruction of which would curb enemy movements on the ground and in the air. He followed the order grudgingly, keen to resume the area bombing of cities instead.

By October, the Allied air forces enjoyed almost total air superiority and German fighter squadrons could only respond when they managed to receive what meagre fuel was available to them. The Command resumed daylight raids, such was its dominance of the skies. In addition, the Germans had been forced to abandon their French-based early-warning systems following the invasion, further hindering their attempts to intercept the Allied bombers.

With ruthless determination, the Allies were throttling the German war machine and bringing it inexorably to a fatal halt.

Mine-laying was carried out by Bomber Command aircraft, as it had been throughout the war. These operations were called "gardening" trips because each area was given a code-name after a flower or vegetable. Mine-laying contributed to the sinking or damaging of over 1,000 enemy ships during the war. U-boat harbours found themselves firmly back on the target-list.

Winter approached and Harris obtained Churchill's agreement to resume area bombing (although he made clear to Harris that he did not believe Bomber Command could "knock Germany flat" on its own without the army), and 60% of all bombs dropped thereafter fell on German cities. Dortmund, Essen and Cologne received further poundings, as did Duisburg, although this city cost the Command many aircraft as a result of its fierce flak defences, mustered even at this late stage in the war. Despite being reminded on several occasions that oil was his primary target, Harris continued to attack cities, citing weather conditions as the determining factor in what his bomber crews' targets were to be. By this stage, even Portal had conceded that bombing alone was not the key to victory.

In November, Bomber Command at last sank the mighty Tirpitz at Tromso. "Operation Catechism" followed previous failed attempts to destroy her. The bombers involved took-off from Scotland. They were significantly modified to allow them to carry the 12,000lb "Tallboy" bomb and reach the Tirpitz's lair far north in the Arctic Circle. The bombs, dropped by 617 "Dambusters" Squadron and 9 Squadron, slammed into the battleship, which rolled over to port in the fjord with the loss of 1,000 sailors.

There was a last-ditch offensive by the Germans in mid-December, when the Sixth SS Panzer Army, having captured some fuel, burst through the Belgian Ardennes Forest and briefly threatened to cut off Montgomery's forces in the north from the Americans in the south. Bad weather initially prevented Bomber Command from going to the aid of the Allies, who had been caught completely off-guard. At last the weather cleared sufficiently for the bombers to help the ground troops and end this unexpected counter-offensive.

Overall, the Allied bombing offensive in 1944 had gone well and by early the following year, German oil production had been reduced to a trickle. But it was the concerted bombing raids on the enemy's transport systems which proved to be the biggest factor in slowing down Germany's armaments industries. Railways and canals in the Ruhr were utterly smashed, and coal deliveries so disrupted that steel production collapsed to half the minimum required to maintain the industry.

February 1945 saw the fire-bombing of Dresden. This medieval city in the east of Germany was specifically identified by Churchill to hinder the German retreat from the Soviet advance in the East. Leipzig, Berlin and Chemnitz were also selected for bombing. Dresden was packed with refugees fleeing the Allied bombing campaign on one side and the advancing Russians on the other. There were also thousands of Allied POWs in the city and its environs. The first wave of aircraft dropped incendiaries. The second wave of bombers, whose crews could see the light from the burning city from 200 miles away, dropped blast bombs, the better to spread the flames. Further incendiaries were dropped to catch the fire-fighters as they battled in the streets.

A wireless operator taking part in a raid on the oil refineries at Rositz the following night witnessed the glow as Dresden still burned 50 miles away. American B-17s had continued the assault on Dresden during the day – almost superfluously. Eventually, burning rubble was all that remained of a city which burned for a week and where up to 50,000 people were killed. Concern and outrage at this attack were voiced in America and Britain, but were almost immediately overshadowed by events as Belsen concentration camp was liberated. This came as a sharp reminder of what the Nazis were capable, and criticism of the Dresden raid was more restrained for a time.

On 30 April, Hitler committed suicide in his Berlin bunker. The Germans surrendered on 8 May, although the Japanese capitulation would not be forthcoming until 15 August, with her official surrender on 2 September.

During the course of the war, Bomber Command's raids forced the enemy to draw heavily on its manpower – some estimates say as many as one and a half million men – to defend its cities and industries from aerial onslaught. Although not taken directly from the military's ranks, being mostly older men and youngsters (and slaves), these men could nonetheless have been otherwise employed in Germany's war production. Successful and accurate bombing, particularly towards the end of the war in the spring of 1945, finally choked the enemy's fuel and armaments supplies which had been seriously threatened since as early as 1941.

A truce was agreed with the Germans, who still controlled large areas of Holland, so that food supplies could be dropped by Bomber Command to the starving Dutch people. During "Operation Manna", 6,684 tons of food were dropped in this enormous humanitarian effort.

Although it incurred appalling losses of aircrew, the entire bombing campaign amounted to less than 10% of Britain's war effort. Furthermore, it was a campaign that enjoyed the wholehearted support of the majority of the British population. There were, however, a growing number of voices, including MPs, who expressed grave concern over the morality of bombing cities and civilians. Dresden in particular was seen by many as a sign that Britain had overstepped the mark at a point when the outcome of the war was no longer in any doubt.

For her part, Germany recognised too late the enormous part that the RAF's and the USAAF's heavy bombers played in turning the tide of war. Even when they were staring defeat in the face, the Germans were trying to develop a four-engined bomber that would mirror the RAF's successes, when they should have concentrated their efforts on producing desperately needed fighters to protect their cities from annihilation by Bomber Command.

Many aircraft and their valiant crews contributed to these raids – Stirlings, Halifaxes, Wellingtons, Hampdens and Manchesters amongst them. But it is one aircraft in particular which made its appearance in 1942 and will forever be associated with carrying the war across the North Sea to the Germans, night after night, raining devastating blows upon the enemy far below. Its story began as early as 1939, when the race to design a heavy bomber for the Air Ministry had narrowed to a handful of contenders. All of these produced mock-ups, but only Avro's Manchester was taken further and made into a prototype. 1,200 Manchesters were duly ordered but, in the end, only 200 were actually delivered because of the failure of its design. The Manchester had been designed by Avro's Chief Designer, Roy Chadwick, and was seen to have potential as the heavy bomber sought by the Ministry, but only if significant modifications were implemented. Guy Gibson described the Manchester as being "heavy on the controls", saying that "take off seemed to take hours" and turns were so slow as to be "almost unreal". It suffered continuous problems with its two Vulture engines, which proved to be complex, overloaded and unreliable. The aircraft had a ceiling of 10,000 feet and could not maintain altitude on only one engine. Jokes abounded among Manchester crews of holding their squadron reunions in POW camps and aircrews who flew the Manchester confess that the lack of confidence in its engines meant being airborne was not an experience they relished.

Roy Chadwick was a perfectionist, and modifications to the unreliable Manchester were carried out throughout 1940, with the first test-flight of the re-designed Manchester taking place on 9 January 1941. The improved aircraft had retained the fuselage and wing centre-section. The central tail fin had been removed, and the remaining twin tail planes and their fins and rudders had been increased in size. The overall wingspan was enlarged. Gone were the two woefully underpowered Vulture engines; in their place were four immense Merlins. The aircraft received favourable reports from test pilots and had successful trials in the air. The revised aircraft was officially called the Avro Type 683 and then the Manchester III, but the designers had for some time been calling her by another name altogether, the one by which she was to become universally known.

She was a mighty aircraft, the like of which had never been seen before – a fearsome warrior of the skies who was waiting to take her place in history and in the heart of a nation.

She was called the Lancaster.

Chapter Five

"THE SHINING SWORD"

Harris christened the Lancaster his "Shining Sword". A more formidable aircraft at the time would be hard to imagine and to many she remains the supreme instrument of victory in the Second World War. Airmen said that, if you flew Lancasters, they reckoned that you had "made it". She retains their unstinting admiration and affection.

The first three Lancasters were introduced to 44 (Rhodesia) Squadron at Waddington on Christmas Eve 1941, their first operational flight taking place in January. Angela Nall, whose father, Alec Coryton, was AOC No. 5 Group at this time, recalls him coming into their drawing room in Grantham and announcing, "The first Lancs have arrived!", with great excitement.

So much hope was placed in this new bomber ... yet she more than lived up to expectations. Within a year Bomber Command deployed eighteen squadrons of these huge aircraft, the number rising to 57 by April 1945. 7,366 Lancasters were built during the war.

The Lancaster's sole purpose was to carry as many bombs as fast and as far as possible to the enemy – and drop them. To this end, she was designed to hoist an incredible all-up weight of 60,000lbs, comprising her airframe, fuel, crew, armaments and, of course, bombs. Her maximum speed was 310 mph whilst flying at

21,000 feet. She was straightforward to fly and could remain stable even when badly damaged.

When stationary, the Lancaster sat at an angle with her nose raised, as though watching the skies. Her sleek lines and neat appearance disguised her strength and capacity to carry immense bombs. She was covered in light alloy skin, apart from her ailerons which were fabric-covered. Bomber Command's Lancasters were painted dull black on their undersides to help them blend in with the night skies and disguise them from the enemy trying to spot them from the ground; their topside was camouflaged. The alloy skin was just that – a skin. Of necessity, it was lightweight and therefore offered scant protection from flak and none at all from an enemy fighter's 20mm cannon shells. There was one pair of 7mm thick armored doors in the bulkhead of the fuselage and a single armour-plated shield behind the pilot's head; otherwise the crew was at the mercy of whatever the enemy chose to throw at them.

She was a utility machine; there was nothing superfluous contained within her. Inside, she was very stark and austere: pipes, cables and wiring, carrying power and hydraulic fluid, were all visible running like arteries along the walls of her interior. Handrails ran along either side inside the fuselage; they were vital for enabling the crew to move around the aircraft whilst she was flying. On the port side of the middle section of fuselage was a rest couch for injured crew. Further back along the fuselage were stored ammunition boxes for the gunners, marine distress signals, a fireman's axe, the First Aid kit, the access ladder used to climb in and out, (stowed during flight), the Elsan sanitary toilet pan and twelve thermos flasks. The flare chute was on the floor of this part of the aircraft. The main entrance was on the starboard side of the rear fuselage.

The aircraft was sparsely furnished because every pound in weight counted: the size of the bomb load she could carry was the Lancaster's entire reason for being. As one American serviceman commented when inspecting a Lancaster for the first time, she was "just one Goddamn flying bomb-bay". She was the only Allied bomber capable of heaving the 22,000lb Grand Slam deep-penetration bomb into the air. The bomb bay was cavernous and stretched for more than thirty feet along her belly, from beneath the front of the cabin to behind the wings and almost as far as the mid-upper turret. The usual bomb load comprised one 4,000lb high explosive "Cookie" and twelve SBCs (small bomb containers), each holding many incendiaries, but the precise type and number of bombs depended upon the particular mission. The bomb release sequence was meticulously pre-set before any operation.

Nothing was wasted at all. The tremendous energy generated by her four Merlin engines was not just harnessed for flight: each of the engines was fitted with a 1500 watt generator which provided power for various hydraulic systems pumps. Flaps, brakes, bomb-bay doors, gun turrets and the undercarriage all drew on those engines for their power. If an engine was put out of action, the undercarriage, for example, would then have to be lowered by a hand-operated pump. This painstaking process required fifteen minutes of effort by a crewman.

Looking at her from front to rear, her purpose was evident: to fly fast and to deliver her bombs to the enemy. She had to be able to defend herself against aerial attack, and, finally, to bring her precious crew home again.

Her wings had a span of 102 feet, and their leading edges were reinforced against barrage balloons. Each wing held three self-sealing fuel tanks (she had six tanks in total). If ruptured by shellfire, the tanks could seal themselves – up to a point – to prevent fuel loss. There were two mighty Merlin engines on each wing.

The starboard wing contained the dinghy, stowed under a panel flush with the wing surface. The dinghy could be released in the event the Lancaster was ditched by pulling a cord inside the aircraft: this would simultaneously inflate the dinghy. (Aircrew who survived ditchings automatically became members of The "Goldfish Club".) A Lancaster came down at Gunthorpe (two miles from Hoveringham) moments after taking off from RAF Syerston in 1943, when its dinghy accidentally released itself and became entangled around the tail section of the aircraft, rendering it unflyable. It went into a steep descent whilst the pilot battled to maintain level flight, before it crashed and exploded near Glebe Farm. All the crew were killed.

The Lancaster's massive wings were connected to each other by the main wing spar, which passed across and through the fuselage. The crew had to climb over this spar each time they made their way forward or aft through the plane. Clambering over the spar in flying gear has been described by airmen as "nothing less than an obstacle course". Beneath the wings, the two enormous main wheels were shoulder height, their size reflecting the phenomenal weight they had to bear.

At the very tail-end of the aircraft was the backwards-facing rear gun turret bristling with four .303 Browning machine guns and flanked by the reassuring twin tail fins. A single small tail-wheel supported the rear of the aircraft whilst it was stationary or taxi-ing. As the Lancaster gathered speed along the runway, the tail rose elegantly into the air and the turret was lifted from the ground, the aircraft fuselage horizontal in the moments before take off.

But this magnificent aircraft needed a crew to guide her to the enemy far below in the darkness. It is all too easy to forget that there were seven men in every single Lancaster that took to the skies.

Chapter Six

THE CREW

Each Bomber Command airman was "above average intelligence", wrote Harris in his memoirs. They had to be, to cope with the daunting task that lay ahead. Having joined up, these eager young men were sworn in, sworn at, innoculated and subjected to stringent medical checks. Their eyes and lungs had to be near-perfect (one nervous volunteer held his breath so long that he had to be told to breathe by the alarmed Medical Officer). Their teeth were also of particular interest to the selection board: anyone with bad fillings or an abscess would suffer at altitude as the reduced air pressure allowed the slightest fissure or hole in a tooth to expand and cause excruciating pain. A distraction like toothache was hardly desirable when trying, for example, to plot wind speed and a new course at 20,000 feet. Sinus problems would also cut short many an airman's career and one or two were known to pass out at altitude despite having their own oxygen supply: they were moved to other branches of the RAF.

The crew of a Lancaster comprised a pilot, flight engineer, bomb-aimer, navigator, wireless operator, mid-upper gunner and rear gunner. Each man specialised in his particular field, and received training of the highest order. They had to take multiple tests, and a strong grasp of mathematics was a priority. At the outset of their training, the men were grouped with others learning the same skill.

Pilots learned to fly in Tiger Moths, Miles Magisters or similar aircraft with varying standards in instruction. One young trainee pilot (who later flew in Lancasters) was about to take off for a solo flight in a Tiger Moth and anxiously asked his instructor at what point he should pull the stick back before landing. The answer (not very helpfully) was: "When you can see the blades of grass!" Trainee pilots proceeded to twin-engined aircraft such as Airspeed Oxfords or Avro Ansons. After an average of 130 hours' flying instruction, they received their pilot's wings and were ready to move on to Wellingtons at Operational Training Units.

Trainee bomb-aimers, navigators and wireless operators attended lectures and took part in exercises relevant to their subjects such as radio transmission, radar, aircraft recognition, navigation (including taking astro-shots with an astrocompass – not easy from a turret in a vibrating aircraft) and meteorology. They were tested at every stage to make sure they were "up to the job". As a reminder that they were in the armed forces, all the men had to do their "left, right, left, right" – as one pilot described drill.

Air gunners attended gunnery school where they were given shotguns and taught to shoot clays in order to learn about hitting moving targets, before progressing onto the Browning machine guns that would become their companions in the air. The gunners' skill was not easy to master and is sometimes overlooked. Anyone who has tried to shoot a moving target will comprehend something of the difficult challenge they faced. They had to master the effect on bullets of gravity drop, the wind and the forward speed of the aircraft, all of which affected the crossing speed of a bullet to its target (the "time and flight" of the bullet). Gunners had to be able to calculate an enemy fighter's range and speed in a matter of seconds; often the most they had to go on was a glimpse as it raced in for the kill. "Fighter affiliation" sessions entailed each gunner taking it in turns to sit in the rear turret and aim at chasing Spitfires or Hurricanes, so that they could familiarise themselves with the theory of "curve and pursuit" which aptly described how a fighter attacked. Air-sickness was a big problem for some of the newcomers, and it was often a relief to vacate the turret and let the next man have a go. Other lessons involved firing at drogues towed behind tug planes, using live ammunition. There were lots of aircraft taking part in this type of exercise at any one time, so each gunner had different coloured marker bullets; back on the ground, it was then apparent who had hit and who had missed the drogue.

Up until this point, the men were not formed into actual crews, and had only mixed with others on the same courses as themselves, so navigators had only come across navigators and bomb-aimers other trainee bomb-aimers. This was all about to change.

"Crewing up" took place once they had completed – and passed – these initial training courses and had been sent to OTUs at airbases: it was, and remains, one of the most bizarre and haphazard methods of allocating men to a team. Hundreds of airmen would be assembled in a hangar and told to "get on with it", milling around and trying to see which crew still required a navigator, or which pilot had a good training record – or not. In this noisy melee would be British, Canadian, New Zealand, Australian and South African airmen, and this mixture of nationalities was then reflected in the crews. Once a crew had come together, it stayed together, throughout the rest of the training course and into the men's posting to operational squadrons. Established crews were only broken up by illness, injury or death.

Some aircrew likened this peculiar rigmarole to selecting partners at a dance – looks could be deceptive and there was no guarantee that someone was not going to tread on your toes. Basically, pilots were seeking four men to form the nucleus of a crew: a bomb-aimer, navigator, wireless operator and rear gunner. (Mid-upper gunners and flight engineers were not required at this stage, only making their appearance once the novice crews graduated finally to Heavy Conversion Units (HCUs) where they learned to fly "heavies" and a correspondingly bigger crew was required.)

One wireless operator recalls ending up in a crew with a gunner who was in his mid-thirties. The unfortunate gunner was regarded with suspicion because of his "rheumy eyes" and his age (anyone over twenty-five naturally being considered elderly by airmen whose average age was twenty-one) and the rest of the crew were relieved to see him replaced by a younger man soon afterwards.

It was nigh on impossible to gauge your future bomb-aimer's ability from, say, his face or his shoe size, but first impressions still counted for a lot. When you were about to go to war and place your life in the hands of complete strangers, trust in each other was going to be paramount. There was a lot of luck involved, but a great many surviving crews became firm friends and remain so to this day.

Training intensified from here on, with the men now regarded as a team. The aircraft that they were now flying were Wellingtons and Stirlings, which had played a large part early in the Bomber Offensive but which were now relegated to training duties as bigger aircraft began to be used by operational squadrons.

The crew's faith in each other, centred on the pilot, was growing each day. Depending on which base, accommodation could vary from Nissen huts – where one navigator described conditions as rather like living in a "leper colony, miles away from the main base" – to purpose-built brick H-block aircrew quarters. A former wireless operator remembers a Nissen hut being boarded up at his airfield near Lincoln, because the crew allocated to it repeatedly encountered the ghost of an airman inside and refused to enter it after a while.

Crews kept themselves to themselves and, although it was considered acceptable for pilots to socialise with other pilots, by and large it was regarded as vaguely disloyal for a rear-gunner to spend too much time in the company of another crew's pilot, for example. This closeness of a crew became more acute once they were actually flying on operations: as one wireless operator recalls, "you looked after your own mates in the air – that was it". These little groups were fiercely loyal amongst themselves, but as one admits, where girls were concerned, it was "every man for himself!"

The men attended many hours at ground school, as well as flying. The pilot, having progressed to Wellingtons, would be flying on dual and solo flights (i.e., with an instructor and without) and on the little Link Trainer (similar to a modern-day simulator) in ground school which was an invaluable aid. He would practice landing the Wellington with only one engine, with flaps and without flaps, on beam approach and much more. All these exercises would then be repeated at night. It was an exhaustive process.

After two or three weeks, the fledgling crews were posted to an HCU, where they began their association with "heavies" such as Stirlings or Halifaxes ("Halibags"). The precious Lancasters were not yet within their reach: they would only be let loose on them during the final stages of training; these bombers were required on the front line and could not be spared for training until the crews were more proficient.

Cross-country flights, night exercises and practice runs over local bombing ranges were carried out regularly until they became second nature to the men; these flights involved all the crew although the rear gunner, who had little to do except admire the vanishing countryside below, sometimes complained of feeling like a passenger.

To complete their training, the crews were posted to a Lancaster Finishing School (LFS) where, at last, they were introduced to the magnificent aircraft that they would be entrusted to fly. It is apparent from diaries and letters that airmen adored these aircraft. "We were all happy with this champion," said one pilot. "It was top of the shops," recalls another. Whilst at LFS, the crew met their flight engineer and mid-upper gunner for the first time. Rear gunners and mid-upper gunners would put their heads together to devise tactics for when they would have to face enemy aircraft.

Now a team of seven, the crew's training intensified and became totally focused on the Lancaster. All the men learned the basics of each other's jobs, with varying levels of success. As one wireless operator admitted, the "flight engineer bit was beyond me". Time and again, the men practised negotiating the interior of the aircraft in the dark and baling out. Dinghy practice was carried out in a pool (airmen based at airfields close to Lincoln used a school swimming pool in the city centre). Many are the airmen who would thank their lucky stars that these rehearsals were as thorough as they had been – it would save their lives in the real event.

Although somewhat cocooned at LFS, the young trainee crews could not avoid details reaching them of the horrendous losses being suffered by operational squadrons; dreadful though these were, the new crews were nonetheless keen to be initiated into the front line. It was, after all, what they had joined up to do.

Long cross-country flights became commonplace, and a trip to Scotland and back was not unusual. Bombing practice was carried out on local ranges: live ammunition was used on the range at Wainfleet off the Lincolnshire coast (still an MOD bombing range today). Closer to RAF Syerston, the quiet village of Epperstone was home to its own bombing range. Epperstone bombing range was used by LFS crews, as well as already-operational squadrons honing their skills. Villagers still recall the thunder of Lancasters coming over the hills at all hours of the day and night to drop their bombs on the target, and one villager said it was not a pleasant experience to be cycling along nearby lanes in total darkness, wondering whether she was going to be hit by a stray bomb.

The target at Epperstone was described by a former navigator as a large white triangle roughly twenty feet across. It was situated in a field near a stream at the bottom of a valley. In nearby fields stood a pair of quadrant towers, several hundred yards apart and up the valley from the target. The spotters in the towers would take a reading on where the bomb had fallen, and the accuracy of the Lancaster crew would be recorded and reported back to the crew's unit. The whole set-up was manned round-the-clock by the RAF.

Smoke bombs were used during the day and flash bombs at night: neither were "live" ammunition but, nonetheless, these bombs managed to inflict damage. The farmer whose fields had been requisitioned by the RAF for this range describes smoke bombs landing in the cow shed, the orchard beside the farmhouse, and other locations entirely unplanned by the Air Force. The bombs whistled as they fell, and left round holes where they entered the ground. His father always told him that, if he were caught in the open fields as the Lancasters approached, to run and stand on the actual target, because "they'll *never* hit you there!" The bombs were about eighteen inches long, and the fields were peppered with many thousands of them. After the war, when sugar beet was grown in those fields, the bombs were inevitably dug up along with the beet, causing havoc at the sugar factory in Newark. To this day, although the two towers and the target are long gone, the fields they stood in are still called "RAF 1", "RAF 2" and "RAF 3" by the farmer.

Meanwhile, at the Lancaster Finishing School, anticipation mounted as the course neared its conclusion and the day approached when the crews would be posted to their operational squadrons. They were desperately impatient, after all their many months of training, to get their own chance to strike a blow at the enemy across the Channel.

No 5 LFS was but one of several finishing schools in the country and its home was RAF Syerston, one of the better-known bomber bases in England. This veteran bomber station witnessed more than its fair share of supreme heroism and absolute, wretched tragedy. The airmen who were to die at Hoveringham in January 1945 were just some of the many who took off on a flight from this airfield, but did not return.

Chapter Seven

RAF SYERSTON

At the beginning of the war, it cost just over £500,000 to build an RAF bomber station; it cost almost twice as much by the end of the war as airfields grew in sophistication and size. These were massive undertakings and, between 1938 and 1946, over 550 new military airfields were built, taking the total in Britain to well over 700. In 1942 alone, 60,000 men were employed solely in airfield construction around the country, with work starting on a new airfield every three days. It was the biggest engineering feat since the railways had been built in the nineteenth century and it was a very necessary one. To get thirty bombers into the air in an hour, no fewer than 3,000 officers and men were required on a bomber station.

An average of 700 to 1,000 acres of flat ground was required for an airfield and, in the late 1930s, the Air Ministry had their eye on a perfect site for their new bomber station, six miles south-west of Newark and ten miles north-east of Nottingham. This was farmland belonging to the Flintham estate (owned by the Hildyard family of Flintham Hall). The new airfield was named after the nearby village of Syerston and was in a dramatic location. It was bounded by the main A46 Leicester to Newark road (the dead straight Fosse Way, dating from Roman times) on its southern side and the near-vertical wooded escarpment that falls away down to the River Trent on its northern side. The road and the river left little room for error on the part of pilots, but the height of the main runway above the river plain below – approximately 150 feet – gave the aircraft an altitude advantage on take-off to the south-west. Syerston suffered from a notorious downdraught at this end of the airfield, which caused at least two serious aircraft crashes with fatalities, but the overall height gained made this risk worthwhile. The north-east end of the main runway is markedly higher than the surrounding countryside.

The Flintham estate had three farms on the proposed site: two were demolished and a third, Trent Hills Farm, was taken down and rebuilt in its present location just outside the airfield boundary, where it was daubed with camouflage paint to match the disguise of the other airfield buildings. Ancient tracks, such as Long Hedge Lane which led to the river were obliterated; hedges and trees were removed wholesale. The perimeters of the airfield had a good deal of mature woodland and, as the airfield grew in size, hangars and various other buildings were dispersed throughout these woods, to aid their concealment.

Syerston was one of the last permanent airfields to be built before the war, following the RAF's expansion period of the mid-thirties. It opened on 1 December 1940 as one of the operational bomber stations of No.1 Group Bomber Command, under the command of Group Captain Sanderson.

Initially, there was confusion amongst Air Force personnel posted to Syerston, as the rail warrants issued to them were persistently made out to Bleasby station. On the map, this is indeed the nearest railway station; in reality it is across the River Trent from the airfield and a ten mile drive away from it, via the nearest bridge at Newark. Despite repeated reminders from Syerston to the Air Ministry, airmen continued to arrive for some time at Bleasby station, where, bemused, they had to await collection by the airfield's transport.

In common with other airfields at that time, RAF Syerston had no designated runways and was merely one enormous grass take-off and landing area. At the outbreak of war, only nine airfields had specific grass runways, and a mere three bomber stations had concrete runways.

To prevent the large grassy area from revealing the airfield's location to the Germans, specialist teams of "camoufleurs" were employed by the Air Ministry to disguise airfields including Syerston: amongst their number were architects, artists and theatre set designers. Ironically, they were commissioned to "paint" open spaces to make them look exactly as they had done before they were requisitioned. Their solution was to spray black bituminous emulsion paint directly onto the grass to imitate hedges, trees and shadows, and to break up the runway area to resemble fields. Silicate paints were used on concrete and cement, although even when painted a concrete runway was still highly visible to reconnaissance aircraft at over 5,000 feet, and particularly so in the rain when it became shiny. Other methods of camouflaging the concrete were therefore tried: coloured slag or chipped stone led to unsustainable numbers of punctures on aircraft; experiments were also made with sawdust, woodchip, pebbles and even seaweed; but in the end, it was wood chip which got the vote as the most successful (coloured paint was then sprayed onto the chips). Seeding and mowing on a huge scale was employed after 1941 and agricultural machinery found a novel use altogether as an aid to airfield subterfuge. After 1943, airfield camouflage became focused almost exclusively on the eastern counties of Britain.

As an extra deception, there was a decoy airfield at the village of Kneeton, less than two miles away. This decoy even had its own generator to power lights in an attempt to lure enemy bombers away from the genuine bomber station. False runways and buildings featured at these decoy airfields, which could be found at many locations across England. As the threat of Luftwaffe air raids diminished after 1943, the decoy airfields were gradually abandoned back to nature.

The first squadrons to arrive at Syerston in December 1940 were 304 and 305 Polish bomber squadrons flying Fairey Battles. Whilst at Syerston, these airmen learned to operate Wellingtons. Once they had completed their conversion to these bombers, they carried out their first raid in Wellingtons in April 1941, against petrol and fuel oil storage tanks in Rotterdam.

There were four Polish bomber squadrons in Nottinghamshire and several Polish training units. Ferocious fighters, the Poles were intent on taking to the skies at any cost to attack the Germans, even undertaking extra tours. Many (particularly fighter pilots) were already veterans after coming up against the Luftwaffe in Poland. Having seen the fate that had befallen their own country, they knew they had everything to lose if Britain fell too and were fanatical in their loathing of the enemy. "Like little Jack Russell terriers", was how one Syerston resident described them. A British airman at Syerston commented that they were "very brave fighters but their food was awful sloppy stuff". The black market, in particular, thrived during their sojourn at Syerston, with rumours of farmers exchanging food for gasoline. On one occasion at nearby Newton, a fire broke out in a Wellington's engine following a backfire when it was started up by its Polish crew. The fire was quickly extinguished by ground crew and the Poles took off, desperate to join the bomber stream. But the engine had backfired in the first place because the Poles had stuffed their coats into the air intake to speed up the engine start, a somewhat unorthodox method! An RAF flight engineer recalls that Poles "had their own way of doing things" but that they never gave him any cause for alarm, as long as he laid down the rules before taking to the air.

In January 1941, the King and Queen visited the station with Air Chief Marshal Sir Richard Pierse (then Commander-in-Chief, Bomber Command). March 1941 brought a sharp reminder of the war with a German bombing raid of the airfield. Residents in nearby Flintham village heard the ominous drone of approaching German aircraft. George Tindale was a young boy and watched the German planes coming in low over his father's farmyard in the village, to be followed moments later by rapid series of explosions from the direction of RAF Syerston less than a mile away. Ground machine guns and two Armadillo armoured cars fired at the enemy aircraft, which turned and headed back to the coast, unscathed. Nine delayed-action bombs had been dropped, but the raid did little serious damage and the holes in the runway were soon filled in and bulldozed level again.

Later in the war, Syerston was targeted again when a landmine – a high explosive bomb which had a parachute attached to it – fell between Kneeton and East Bridgford; the tremendous blast was heard for many miles around and the large crater is still visible in the field today. Across the river in Hoveringham, several houses suffered shock-wave damage to doors and windows from the blast. The Clarke family lived at Ferry Farm on the opposite bank of the River Trent from the explosion. Their landlord, Trinity College, Cambridge, had painted the woodwork of their house so assiduously that the windows had been sealed shut. The explosion blew them open and the Clarkes could use them properly for the first time in years.

The Poles left Syerston for Lindholme in July 1941, and 408 (Goose) Squadron arrived in their place. Syerston was transferred to No. 5 Group Bomber Command at this time. 408 Squadron was a Canadian unit which brought old Handley Page Hampdens with them and they flew their first mission in August: like the Poles before them, Rotterdam was their first target. Maurice Ashby, a young boy from Flintham, crawled through the perimeter hedge with a friend, and the two boys climbed into one of the Hampdens waiting on its dispersal. In due course, the ground crew arrived to prepare it for the evening operation and found the two boys, who were then sent off with an expletive. (Maurice admits to having felt increasingly alarmed that he was going to be trapped in the aircraft and accompanying the crew on a raid.)

In December 1941, this squadron transferred to nearby Balderton airfield while Syerston was enlarged and modified to accommodate the "heavies" – in particular Lancasters – which were starting to be introduced to bomber squadrons. Concrete runways, with additional length, were going to be needed at every single bomber station, as well as extended cleared areas at both ends of the runway. (As early as 1937, the Commander-in-Chief of Bomber Command,

Air Chief Marshal Sir Edgar Ludlow-Hewitt had foreseen the problems with grass-only runways and commented ruefully that his force "would only be able to operate in dry weather!" unless the airfields were significantly improved.) In particular, Syerston tended to have a high water table after continuous rain, despite extensive under-draining.

Accordingly, during the winter and spring of 1941–42, Syerston underwent a major transformation and had three runways put down in the shape of a letter A, in common with all other "Class A" airfields at that time. The main runway was aligned on a north-east/south-west bearing to harness the prevailing winds in this country. It was 1,900 yards long, and the other two runways, which joined each other next to the A46, were 1,430 yards in length.

The gravel used in the concrete for the runways was extracted from two rectangular quarries at Hazelford, across the Trent from the airfield. (These quarries are now attractive lakes ringed by willow trees.) The concrete mixer was sited next to Coneygre wood, on the western side of the airfield. Building firms such as George Wimpey and MacAlpine played a large part in airfield construction around the country, as did En Tout Cas, perhaps better known for putting down tennis courts. Bulldozers and steamrollers levelled the length of runway, before the concrete was poured onto it. An enormous machine pulled by a bulldozer then smoothed the concrete, moving at a snail's pace along the entire 1,900 yards.

With Syerston now upgraded to a heavy bomber station, it re-opened for business on 5 May 1942. The airfield came under the protection of the RAF regiment which had been formed on 1 February 1942, and which had taken over airfield guarding duties from the Army. Syerston was a well-protected and secretive place;

only civilians who were employed there had regular access to its day-to-day goings-on.

Like other airfields, Syerston was self-contained, with its own power, underground fuel tanks (these could contain up to 72,000 gallons of aviation fuel each), and water supply. Its back-up generator was housed in the standby-set building located on the other side of the A46. This was a dour windowless brick block protected by double blast-proof walls. Jack Barnet manned the standby-set building in the war and, in the event of a power failure, had explicit orders to start the back-up generator and shut down everything on the airfield except for the control tower, teleprinter, hospital and workshops. The generator was powered by a massive engine which could get so hot that it required its own refrigeration unit in the building to keep it cool.

A perimeter track encircled the airfield, fifty feet wide and nearly three miles long. Leading off this perimeter track at intervals were the circular dispersal areas where the bombers were parked. These dispersals were frying-pan shaped from above, and usually 125–150 feet in diameter. They were loacated as far from each other and the rest of the airfield buildings as possible, in order to make them harder for enemy aircraft to pin-point and destroy in bombing raids. (In the First World War, aircraft were squeezed together in hangars and a single bomb could destroy the lot.) Like most British bomber stations in the Second World War, Syerston had 36 dispersals; American bomber bases required fifty or more.

The A46 was gated and closed to traffic while Lancasters were crossing it to and from the dispersals on the south side of the road, or when aircraft were taking off or landing on one of the shorter runways (the flight path for these being directly over the road).

To a young boy, this was quite a draw and George Tindale used to crouch in a ditch by the road and watch the bombers coming in to land. On one occasion, the tail wheel of a landing Lancaster snagged the perimeter barbed-wire fence nearby his hiding-place; the coils of wire were snatched up into the air before wrenching free and falling back down with a crash. After that incident, he moved further away from the runway.

Giant hangars were erected around RAF Syerston. There were two "J" type hangars, several T2 hangars and one B1 hangar. The "J" type hangars, with curved steel roofs, are all that remain of these cavernous buildings. 300 feet long and with a span of half that distance, they are still very prominent and easily visible from many miles away. The parked aircraft lived outside on dispersals, and only came into a hangar for servicing or repair, when the aircraft would be towed to the mouth of the hangar. The order "Two Six!" would then be called out by the sergeant in charge, instructing the ground crew to push the bomber backwards inside the hangar. "It was all hands on deck – they were heavy planes," recalls one former ground crew man. The hangars contained workshops, and as much of the preparation for the aircrafts' missions was done inside as possible. The batteries, for instance, were charged inside the hangars before being taken out to the waiting aircraft. However, re-fuelling (it could take half an hour to fill up a Lancaster's 2,100 gallon tanks), topping up the oil, and arming the aircraft were all done at the dispersal, whatever the weather.

A great many ground crew (or "erks" as they were nicknamed – supposedly from the Cockney pronunciation of the abbreviation of "aircraftman", or "airc") risked pneumonia and frostbite as a result of their work maintaining the bombers on these bleak, windswept dispersals, often in freezing weather conditions. The wartime winters, especially the early years of the war, were particularly harsh and it required tremendous effort by all station personnel to keep runways, dispersals and aircraft free of snow. Everyone, aircrews included, were expected to help shovel snow when required: "It's your bloody aircraft!" was one erk's retort to a member of the aircrew. Apart from their little ground crew huts located at each dispersal, the erks were terribly exposed to the elements. Their huts were an engineering science in their own right, fashioned from corrugated iron, wooden planks and tarpaulins and air crews recognized it as an honour to be invited in for a brew or a game of cards.

Centrally placed and overlooking the runways was the control tower. Two stories high, this building featured large windows on all sides; it had a railed balcony on the first floor and railings on the roof which served as a further vantage point. This was the hub of the entire airfield and housed the flying control and weather offices. It was crammed with radio equipment and also contained the teleprinter, a vital piece of equipment which received operational orders from Group HQ (it was, however, silenced on one occasion when Italian POWs clearing trees near the airfield somehow felled the telegraph pole carrying its wires).

Two large white letters displaying the airfield's unique wartime identification code were visible to pilots in the sky. At night, the letters were flashed in red, in Morse code. (Trainee pilots had to learn the various codes to identify different airfields from the air.) These letters were flashed from various points around the airfield, up to one or two miles away. George Hall was an erk at Syerston who specialised in electrical maintenance and was often sent to man these beacons. He was responsible for changing the codes daily and had a basic caravan for his accommodation.

Every airfield had many administrative buildings and technical sites, such as the armoury and vehicle repair shops. The operations room was placed well away from the main site, as was the Officers' Mess where the pilots were billeted (pilots were precious: a direct hit from a bomb would have put a virtual stop to the airfield's activities). Maurice Ashby's father was the stoker at the Officers' Mess, and arranged for the village blacksmith in Flintham to fashion a three-pronged fork, resembling a trident, with which the officers could make their toast in the stoke-hole at the Mess. Adjacent to the Officers' Mess were their garages and the squash court, which was popular with many officers including Guy Gibson who was a regular player.

Dispersed in the surrounding countryside were further accommodation huts, mess halls, communal buildings and sick quarters. Nissen huts sprouted like mushrooms in every direction; there were many in the densely wooded grounds of Flintham Hall, housing aircrew and ground crew. (Today only one remains standing, although the outlines of others can just be discerned in the gloom of the woods, testament to the thriving community that once lived there.) Some were erected as far away as Syerston village and ground crews were billeted there. Once the vast sprawl of the airfield is taken into account, it becomes apparent why a bicycle was such an integral part of an airman's life.

Most Bomber Command airmen seemed to know where Syerston was, even if they were not stationed there. It was a popular posting for a variety of reasons. Amongst its virtues were the comfortable brick-built accommodation for many of the aircrew, the relaxed and friendly atmosphere, the good food and also (this is mentioned most often!) the close proximity of Nottingham for a night out. One airman who was stationed there described hitching a lift or catching Mr. Gash's bus into the city, and a truck being dispatched from the airfield in the early hours of the following morning to "shovel what was left of the men up" and return them to Syerston. Ron Mather, a wireless operator on Lancasters, offered a bed for the night to one or two other airmen as his family home was (conveniently) in Nottingham. Explaining to his mother the following morning why there were eighteen airmen sleeping in her front room was another matter.

The Sergeants had their own mess. Erks and WAAFs queued together in other ones. The dining hall at Syerston was huge and could seat 650 men; furthermore it had to operate around the clock to reflect the twenty-four hour life of a bomber airfield. The catering at Syerston is immortalised by one airman who wrote in his diary: "Grub very good and ultra clean," after arriving from another airfield. He also added that the "station dance was wizard and there are some wizard WAAFs here!"

The camp cinema was situated in the woods at Flintham Hall, and comprised an extra long Nissen hut with an aisle flanked by wooden chairs. It was an extremely popular venue both for airmen and the villagers from Flintham, who were allowed to frequent it too (it was far cheaper than the cinema in Newark). The pilot of one of the Lancasters that crashed at Hoveringham wrote in his last letter home that the weather was so bad (it being January), his crew had confined themselves to going to the camp cinema, rather than attempting to cycle through snow to the local pubs or trying to go into Nottingham.

Roy Hill, who was a wireless operator, was based at Syerston for a while and remembers watching "Strike up the Band" (starring Judy Garland) in the camp cinema, when the lights suddenly came on and all aircrew were ordered back to the main base for flying duties. He recalls wryly, "I never did see the end of that film".

The bomb stores and ammunition dumps were, for obvious reasons, well away from everything, and situated on the north side of the airfield near the River Trent.

In May 1942, the first incumbents of the re-furbished RAF Syerston, 61 Squadron, arrived from Woolfox Lodge further south down the A1 where they had already converted from Manchesters to Lancasters. They embarked on numerous bombing raids from Syerston to cities including Hamburg, Bremen and Dusseldorf. On 30 May, aircraft from this squadron took off from Syerston to participate in the first thousand-bomber raid to Cologne, and residents of Hoveringham and Kneeton experienced the indescribable roar as, one by one, the Lancasters started their engines and then thundered over the village to join the hundreds of other aircraft already airborne. "I remember them standing out against a mackerel sky", recalls one villager. Jack Barnet was a young boy living with his grandmother at the Old Vicarage at Kneeton and remembers the willow pattern crockery rattling violently on the dresser. "Sleep was totally impossible", explains another resident. "My mother used to say 'Ey-up, they're off again' ".

In September, 61 Squadron was joined by 106 Squadron which came from RAF Coningsby, and Syerston became a two-squadron operational base. The Station Commander at that time was Group Captain Augustus ("Gus") Walker who is remembered by everyone, Serviceman and civilian alike, with fondness and admiration. His even temperament was well-suited to dealing with the impatient but remarkable character who was commanding 106 Squadron at that time, Wing Commander Guy Gibson.

During this period, Syerston was one of the busiest bomber bases in the country. Many raids were carried out by the two resident Lancaster squadrons, and tales abound of both horror and heroism from these missions. Both squadrons had been practicing low altitude flying since their arrival at Syerston, and proceeded to mount an audacious low-level attack on the Schneider Armament and Locomotive works at Le Creusot in France on 17 October. Guy Gibson led the raid (ten of the 95 aircraft from 5 Group which took part were from his 106 Squadron).

This persistent low-level flying, along the River Trent valley and further afield across the country, was alarming for some villagers, prompting Lady Dowson, who lived close to the river at Brackenhill (half a mile from Hoveringham) to pen a letter to Group Captain Walker at RAF Syerston. She commented that the Lancasters were "rather frightening" and "terribly close" to her house. By return, she received a brusque note from him stating that he was very sorry, but "…there is a war on, you know!"

The aircrews from Syerston were frequent visitors to Hoveringham's pubs, the River Trent posing no obstacle whatsoever to reaching the popular drinking dens on the opposite side. The usual route involved cycling to Kneeton (frequently two airmen to a bike, one balanced precariously over the back wheel), where the bikes were left in Neale's farmyard, next to St. Helen's Church which gazes down on Hoveringham. The rough track, known as Gypsy's Lane, winds down through the woods from the village of Kneeton to the riverbank and is exceedingly steep; the bikes were left at the top to save having to push them back up on the return trip. Occasionally a natty sports car was seen parked in the farmyard amongst the bikes.

At the bottom of Gypsy Lane, the airmen strolled in groups across a grassy plain to a point on the river bank opposite the Old Elm Tree pub, where they "yelled and hollered" for the landlord, Norman Keating, to row his boat across and fetch them. Norman Clarke was a young boy at Ferry Farm, next door to the pub, and watched the airmen from his bedroom window. "They made a terrible racket until they were collected in the boat and rowed across", he remembers. Keating's little boat was crammed with an impossible number of airmen on every crossing and often looked far from safe as it negotiated the current. There were hundreds of airmen and he was rowing across the river so many times that he eventually obtained a larger boat with an engine. There were many soakings from tumbles into the river and at least one airman reportedly drowned, but nonetheless they flocked to Hoveringham.

Girls came from miles away in all directions, and the dances at the Elm Tree have passed into local lore for the sheer numbers of people in the ballroom, which sported a sprung floor and a raised platform where bands played. Sid Crowder was a Hoveringham teenager who comments: "What chance did us local lads have with the girls, with all those uniforms for them to pick from?" Airmen would be sprawled on the river bank in their droves on summers' evenings, and would also walk up Boat Lane to Hoveringham's other hostelries, the Reindeer and the Marquis of Granby on Main Street. Jane Gates lived on Boat Lane and remembers the airmen stopping to chat over the garden wall; she and her parents got to know several of them quite well. Occasionally her parents would ask after the whereabouts of someone; the reply, too often, was: "oh, he bought it". No further explanation was needed.

On the wall at Manor Farm Corner, the names of airmen (and villagers) have been scratched into the bricks. Sergeant Lawrence McElroy was a Canadian airman who carved his name and the date into the wall in 1944. Shortly afterwards, he was shot down over Holland and, very badly injured, was taken to a Dutch hospital and became a POW. He died in Canada in the seventies.

The return climb up Gypsy Lane to retrieve the bicycles from Kneeton was a challenge, to say the least, for inebriated airmen. Ron Mather made it as far as St. Helen's Church on one occasion and spent the rest of the night asleep on a tombstone. Another airman spent hours blundering around in the dark woods on the river bank below Kneeton, hopelessly disorientated.

On 8 December, twelve Lancasters from 61 Squadron and eleven from 106 Squadron took part in a raid on Turin. Drama and tragedy struck at dusk before the bombers had even left the runway, when Gus Walker and Guy Gibson noticed from their vantage point in the control tower that one of the 61 Squadron Lancasters, stationary on the far side of the airfield (near to Syerston Hall and the A46), had somehow opened its bomb bay and disgorged its load of incendiary bombs onto the ground. Some of these were now on fire and at risk of igniting the whole aircraft and, more terrifyingly, its main bomb, the 4,000lb "cookie". Group Captain Walker leapt into a staff car and hared off across the airfield, dodging other taxi-ing Lancasters and ran up to the aircraft, waving his arms to alert the crew on board to the danger developing beneath their aircraft. Gibson had already noticed, however, that the aircraft in question was the reserve one and therefore had no one aboard, but it was too late to stop Walker. The "cookie" bomb suddenly went off and a sheet of flame shot up a couple of thousand feet into the sky. Shrapnel severed Walker's arm below the elbow and caused serious injury to several ground crew. Such was the force of the blast that pieces of the Lancaster's engines were found half a mile away down by the River Trent.

The resulting explosion was clearly heard in Hoveringham, where villagers came out of their houses to see what had caused it; they could see the glow towering up into the sky from across the river Elston Towers, a large mansion on the A46 nearly a mile from the airfield, had every pane of glass blown out of its huge, ornate Victorian conservatory. Jack Barnet watched the entire drama from the airfield itself and, as the "cookie" exploded, flung himself flat on the ground; he said afterwards that he could see the shock wave from the blast racing towards him and then felt it passing over him with a roar.

Incredibly, despite his injury, Gus Walker managed to walk to the ambulance and vowed to be back in command in a month; he was as good as his word and not only returned to RAF Syerston, but continued to fly aircraft and play golf, albeit one-handed (he asked Gibson to look for his severed arm, as he had been wearing a brand-new pair of gloves at the time of the accident).

Public support for, and interest in, the bomber offensive was considerable at this time, and, on 16 January 1943, the BBC War Correspondent Richard Dimbleby was detailed to fly from Syerston in Gibson's Lancaster to report on a raid to Berlin. The trip took a somewhat unexpected turn when Dimbleby passed out on the outward trip. The flight engineer swiftly detected the problem: a

Bicycles everywhere.... a crew make their way to waiting Lancasters on dispersals at RAF Syerston. Photo: Getty Images.

Ground crews fit tailfins to bombs at Skellingthorpe, surrounded by waiting Lancasters. August 1944. Photo: WW2 Images.

As the light fades, a Lancaster prepares to take off, watched by ground crew. Photo: Getty Images.

WAAFs wave off Lancasters from Waddington, 1944. The dalmation puppy which can be seen in the arms of one WAAF used to accompany the crews on their night-flying tests in the mornings.
Photo: Wing Commander Ron Houghton (Retd).

The loneliest eyrie: once he had
pulled his doors closed behind him,
the rear-gunner was totally cut
off from the rest of the crew. His
only means of communication with
them was via the intercom.
Photo: Getty Images.

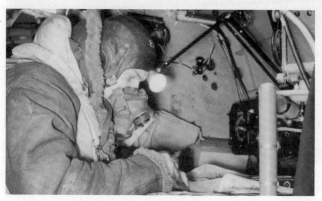

A navigator
at his desk,
14 February
1944.
Photo: WW2
Images.

The mid-upper gunner and his
turret, photographed from the
astrodome. December 1942.
Photo: WW2 Images.

Suspended in his harness, a mid-upper gunner glances down from his
turret, 14 February 1944. Photo: WW2 Images.

Collision, and bombs falling from aircraft above, was a real risk to aircrews. This photo of a daylight raid on 25 April 1945 shows the close proximity of two Lancasters. Photo: WW2 Images.

German Flak gun battery 1940. Photo: WW2 Images.

His turret turned to port as he scans the sky for fighters, the rear-gunner of this Lancaster is unaware of the 500lb bomb about to whistle past his ears. Many aircrew recount stories of near-misses — and impacts, often deadly — from falling bombs. Photo: WW2 Images.

A safe return at dawn, Waddington 1944. Photo: Wing Commander Ron Houghton (Retd), who was the flight engineer in this aircraft.

Guy Dunlop RNZAF (Pilot, JB125, aged 28).
Photo: Dunlop family.

Guy Dunlop's funeral at Oxford Botley
Cemetery, January 1945.
Photo: Dunlop family.

Lancaster lines up with
Syerston over St. Michael's
Church, Hoveringham.

Sgt Patrick Brown RAF (Flight
Engineer, JB125, aged 20).
Photo: Albert Jenkins.

Richard Staples RNZAF
(Wireless Operator, JB125,
aged 23). Photo: Staples family.

Flt Sgt Peter Hill RNZAF
(Navigator, JB125, aged 22),
photographed by his friend,
Albert Evans (Bomb-Aimer).
Photo: John Evans.

Peter Hill and Albert Evans, 1944.
Photo: John Evans.

Peter (left) and Howard,
New Zealand c.1930.
This photograph was
cherished by their
father until his death.
Photo: Helen Whittaker.

Sgt Richard Sedgley RAF
(Rear-Gunner, JB125, aged 19).
Photo: Sedgley family.

Sgt Albert Evans BEM, RAF
(Bomb-Aimer, JB125, aged 26).
Photo: John Evans.

Richard Sedgley's funeral at St. Nicholas's Church, Oddington.
Photo: Sedgley family.

Rathbone was an accomplished artist, as can be seen from this woodcut of a Canadian camping scene.

W/O II Richard Rathbone, RCAF (Pilot, LM308, aged 28). Photo: Donna Johnson.

.... and he had a lively sense of humour, shown in these letter-headings sent to his mother. He drew earwigs in various poses and described his accommodation as "Ear Wig Palace" (it was actually Langar airfield, Nottinghamshire). Courtesy: Donna Johnson.

Albert Mercer and his motorbike, which was admired by other members of his crew. Photo: Pamela Ball/Janice Thorne.

Sgt Albert Mercer RAF (Flight Engineer, LM308, aged 23). Photo: Pamela Ball/Janice Thorne.

Flt Sgt Hugh Mackenzie RCAF
(Navigator, LM308, aged 21).
Photo: MacKenzie family.

Flt Sgt John Emerson RCAF
(Bomb-Aimer, LM308, aged 30).
Photo: Canadian Archives.

Flt Sgt John Reid, (Wireless
Operator, LM308, aged 20), with
his wife Glaidus and infant
daughter Lorna, 1944.
Photo: Lorna Pert (née Reid).

Flt Sgt John Reid RCAF (Wireless
Operator, LM308, aged 20) and
fellow aircrewman, 1944.
Photo: Lorna Pert (née Reid).

Sgt Joseph FitzGibbon RCAF
(Mid-Upper Gunner, LM308,
aged 20).
Photo: FitzGibbon family.

Bill Halley (centre, front
row) and Joseph FitzGibbon
(behind him).
Photo: FitzGibbon family.

Sgt Jasper Martin RAF
(Rear-Gunner, LM308, aged 20).
Photo: Martin family.

Jasper Martin's
funeral, Castleford.
Photo: Martin family.

Only memories remain ... sightless windows overlook fields, where runways once were. Wigsley, Lincolnshire.

Crowds throng to see "Just Jane" at East Kirkby and hear the roar of her mighty Merlin engines, 2009. Photo: author.

kink in their passenger's oxygen tube. When they reached Berlin, Gibson, ever the perfectionist, circled the target three times to make sure of the precise aiming point for his precious 8,000lb "cookie". Dimbleby, who had recovered by now, proceeded to be violently airsick during these protracted manoeuvres. Despite these unfortunate mishaps, Dimbleby completed his report and, when he later broadcast his account of the raid from London, the publicity for not only 106 Squadron, but Bomber Command as a whole was immense.

Gibson's last operation from RAF Syerston with 106 Squadron was to Stuttgart on 11 March 1943. His Lancaster "Admiral Prune" completed the raid with only three engines, one having failed on the outward flight. A boisterous farewell party at the airfield went on into the small hours. He had completed over 170 sorties by this point and had been persuaded to take some long-overdue leave. This was not meant to be, however – he went directly to RAF Scampton to form 617 Squadron and to step into the pages of history by leading the "dambusters" raid on the Mohne, Eder and Sorpe dams two months later. Gibson is well remembered locally and particularly at the Boot and Shoe pub in Flintham, where young George Tindale and his friends were responsible for looking after Gibson's black labrador Nigger (dogs were not allowed in the pub). Gibson would say "just keep an eye on him, lads," and reward the boys later with half a pint of lemonade. Nigger was a familiar sight at the Sergeants' Mess at Syerston on the hunt for food (as Labradors tend to do) or at dispersal awaiting Gibson's return from an operation.

Whilst at Syerston, 61 Squadron saw one of its pilots awarded the Victoria Cross in November 1943, when pilot Flight Lieutenant Bill Reid was injured during an attack by a German night fighter on the outward flight to Dusseldorf. A second attack by another fighter killed his navigator and fatally wounded his wireless operator. The icy gale howling in through Reid's shattered windscreen caused the blood flowing from a head wound to freeze on his skin; nevertheless Reid continued to his destination, dropped his bombs and turned for home, navigating by the pole star and the moon. His flight engineer won a Conspicuous Gallantry Medal for giving Reid, who was passing in and out of consciousness, oxygen from a portable supply. Reid managed to reach England and crash-landed the Lancaster. He recovered from his injuries, but was shot down on a subsequent raid and became a POW.

In November 1943, 106 Squadron left Syerston for Metheringham and 61 Squadron for Skellingthorpe. Syerston ceased to be an operational station and became a training base. It housed 1485 Bombing and Gunnery Flight, which used Wellingtons and Martinets to tow targets for air gunners to use as practice, and also 1690 Bomber Defence Training Flight before it moved to Scampton. In addition, 1668 Heavy Conversion Unit arrived, bringing 18 Lancasters with them. They were to become No. 5 Lancaster Finishing School (LFS).

The No. 5 LFS saw thousands of trainee aircrews pass through its doors en route to operational squadrons. They were usually only at Syerston for a very few weeks while completing their training. This period saw numerous accidents with the loss of many young aircrews who had not seen operational action, as well as valuable instructors who had. Roy Hill, a wireless operator, was typical of a trainee airman: his log book shows that, during their time at Syerston, his crew flew a mere five hours and ten minutes in daylight and six hours at night. That was the *total* extent of their experience in a Lancaster before being sent to face the Luftwaffe and flak defences over Germany, and it was quite normal. The Lancasters available to the young crews had been retired from active service and were "rather dented," Roy recalls. Douglas Jennings, a Lancaster navigator, says that the "wings were liable to come off," if you tried too an aggressive a manoeuvre. There are lurid stories of rivets popping out, but the airmen maintained the highest admiration for the ground crew who kept these battered aircraft airworthy for the training crews.

No. 5 LFS was disbanded on 31 March 1945, the last pupils having passed out the previous month. In April, the airfield became operational again with the arrival of No. 49 Squadron from austere Fulbeck with their Lancasters. This squadron arrived under something of a cloud: traditionally, when a departing squadron took off for its new base, the more high-spirited pilots would "shoot up" the airfield they were leaving, with a brazen low-level fly-past as a final farewell. One of the bombers, PB463, did indeed "shoot up" Fulbeck, but its tail clipped an airfield building and the aircraft came down onto a parade of ground staff from 5015 Works Flight, killing 15 and injuring four. The six airmen on board the aircraft also died in the ensuing fireball. Another pilot waiting to take off commented grimly on the explosion: "So that's how a Lanc goes…" It was a very sombre arrival for the squadron at Syerston.

Forty-nine Squadron took part in only one bombing raid from Syerston, but it was one with inestimable symbolic significance – the destruction of Hitler's lair at Berchtesgarten in Bavaria on 25 April. The dictator's Eagle's Nest and the SS Barracks were levelled to prevent them from becoming places of pilgrimage for Nazi sympathisers. I visited Berchtesgarten as a teenager and can vouch that what 49 Squadron did not succeed in destroying, subsequent souvenir hunters definitely did!

On Monday 7 May 1945, just after tea, the tannoy at Syerston announced that the following day was to be declared Victory in Europe Day: the war in Europe had officially ended. All station personnel enjoyed a lie-in, many only emerging at 10am. There was a parade at the big hangar after lunch with an address by the "Groupie", followed by a service and then Churchill's speech – "In war, resolution, in defeat, defiance, in victory, magnanimity". The sports started and a wagon load of ATS came into the camp. Tea followed the sports and then a station dance in the hangar with cheap beer, but curiously, no glasses. Tins were used instead, and more and more barrels of beer were rolled out from the Sergeants' Mess. Things apparently got quite rowdy and the erks "got tight" (who can blame them?). At the end of the dance, the aircrew turned up the heat and began to drive cars right through the hangar. They also fetched the Very pistols from every aircraft and let them off (Ron Mather ended VE Day with badly singed hair, having been hit on the back of the head with the flare from one of the pistols). The aircrew proceeded to start a big fire in the middle of the parade ground, the flag pole being one of the items burnt with great ceremony, whilst everyone stood around and sang to the music of two accordions.

The celebrations over and hangovers having subsided, 49 Squadron took part in Operation "Exodus", the repatriation of Allied POWs from the continent. There was growing concern that Germany planned to murder all its POWs, prompting the Allies to drop leaflets warning camp commanders and guards that they would be held personally responsible for each prisoner's safety.

Initially, Bomber Command's No. 5 Group undertook the repatriation, whilst No. 1 and No. 3 Groups dropped emergency food supplies over Holland in Operation "Manna", but eventually all the bomber Groups participated in Exodus. Lancasters from 49 Squadron took off from Syerston and flew to Juvincourt, near Reims in France (aircraft from other squadrons also went to Germany and Italy to collect POWs). Each bomber was filled with 25 POWs who were then flown back to England and delivered to Westcott where they were welcomed by WAAFs and cups of tea. The empty 49 Squadron Lancasters then returned to Syerston in preparation for the next trip.

By the end of Operation Exodus on 28 May, 75,000 POWs had been brought back to Britain by Bomber Command's Lancasters, many of the aircrew having volunteered to do these trips. Ron Mather of 49 Squadron recalls that the crew was not issued with parachutes on these missions in a gesture of solidarity with the POWs (who certainly did not have parachutes). The returning POWs were keen to come up to the cockpit and catch their first glimpse of England; Ron, a wireless operator, remembers emotional scenes from men who had spent up to five years incarcerated in prisoner-of-war camps. Many of the POWs were also brandishing assorted souvenirs of dubious origin: German medals, uniforms, swords and pistols.

Syerston's days as a major bomber station were over, but memories remain of the tremendous roar of massed Lancasters as they carried their young crews off into the dark, deadly skies. During the war years, nearly 150 bombers, Hampdens, Manchesters and

Wellingtons amongst them, took off from Syerston and failed to return, but the vast majority of those which were lost – over one hundred and twenty aircraft – were Lancasters.

The airmen of Bomber Command had to put up with jibes about being based in England, where they had access to the home comforts of pubs, cinemas, girls and families. As one wireless operator put it, however, these amenities were mere compensation for the horrors they had to endure nightly on raids. Another bomber crewman responded by simply pointing east to the continent, saying simply, "You fly that-away for two hours or so and you'll find all the war you could ever want".

Chapter Eight

"ALL THE WAR YOU COULD EVER WANT…"

As the first cold fingers of dawn reached above the horizon beyond the Vale of Belvoir, sounds of people and vehicles moving around the airfield at Syerston could be heard. The ghostly mass of the hangars loomed out of the mist and, further away, around the edge of the airfield, the dark forms of Lancasters waited motionless on their dispersals, some half-concealed in woodland clearings, others more exposed on distant dispersals where they formed stark silhouettes against the morning sky.

The ground crews began to carry out routine maintenance and repair to those Lancasters which needed it. Minor repairs were done at the dispersal but the most badly-damaged bombers from the previous night's raid were towed to the yawning entrances of the hangars and worked on inside, sheltered from the elements.

The aircrews who had flown on raids during the night were still asleep, having returned earlier in the small hours from whichever hellish trip they had undertaken. Utterly exhausted, even the noisy goings-on of a busy airfield, such as engines being run up and tested did not intrude upon their sleep. "Insomnia," remembers one wireless operator dryly, "was not something we suffered from".

During the morning, the Station Duty Officer would receive confirmation from Group HQ in Grantham that "ops" would be on that night. He then had to inform a lengthy list of crucial people at Syerston of this fact: the Station Commander, Operations Officers, Intelligence Officers, Senior Navigators and Bomb-Aimers, Meteorological Office, Flying Control, Armoury and Bomb Store, Senior Engineering Officer, Photographic Officers, Mechanical Transport Flight and Senior Mess Staff. The sole purpose of all these people – in fact of the entire airfield – was to get aircraft airborne with their bombs; thereafter all they could do was pray that each one would return safely many hours later in order for the whole exercise to be repeated the following night.

The Squadron Commanders selected crews and aircraft for the raid, and armourers serviced guns and collected fresh ammunition from the Ammunition Stores on the Trent-side of the airfield. By now the aircrews were aware that ops were on for that night, and those crews detailed to operate aircraft were forbidden henceforth from leaving the base. Air-tests were carried out on every bomber due to take part in the raid and frequently the ground crews would accompany the aircrew on these brief flights which aided a close working relationship. A frequent destination for these half-hour air-tests (sometimes called night-flying tests) was Wainfleet off the Lincolnshire coast, where pilots could check their aircraft. As Jim Flint, a Lancaster pilot said, you could: "really woof 'em up". One flight engineer regularly took his dalmation puppy with him on these tests; it would "float around the aircraft with its ears flapping" as the Lancaster experienced negative gravity on dives. The air-tests were completed by lunch, and back at the airfield, full power runs were done on engines, hydraulics, and other systems. The Lancasters were re-fuelled, and crews could gain an inkling of their destination by seeing how much fuel was pumped into the tanks – for instance, 1,850 gallons implied the target was Berlin. The armourers loaded the bombs onto the aircraft, a task which was usually finished by 5 o'clock. The most usual bomb load was a "Cookie" (4,000lb) bomb with either 500lb bombs or incendiaries to a total of approximately 14,000lbs.

The crews, meanwhile, had a long wait until evening, passing the time playing cards, writing letters, reading or resting in an attempt to ignore the mounting tension. Two hours before take-off, they had their main briefing by the Flight Commander or Station Commander in the Briefing Room when they learned their target for that night. The blinds were drawn and station police guarded the door. More specific briefings by each Section leader on navigation, signals, bombing, gunnery and meteorology followed. The intelligence briefing was listened to closely as it gave warnings of flak positions and fighter stations along the route. The crews were isolated from the outside world from this point, and no access to telephones was permitted.

A supper of bacon and eggs (*real* eggs!), beans, tomatoes and fruit juice was served in the mess before the crews made their way to the Locker Room to get dressed. There was an atmosphere of nervous joviality, but it was often so much bluff. The number of men double-checking that they had their lucky charms on them was testament to the undercurrent of fear. New crews, who had a statistically greater chance of being killed, felt particularly anxious.

Having been dropped off at their dispersal by the WAAF driving the crew truck, the pilot signed the ground crew Flight Sergeant's form to acknowledge that he agreed the aircraft was serviceable. Nerves were taut as half an hour or so of standing around chatting, smoking and leg-pulling now followed. Each member of the crew was issued with a Smith and Weston revolver and six bullets (many of the airmen carried the revolvers inside their thick flying boots, embedded in the fleecy lining). For entertainment, these were sometimes drawn out to shoot at empty cigarette packets or tins whilst the flight engineer carried out the numerous external checks on the aircraft. (There were over ninety further checks inside before the engines could be started and yet more before the aircraft could move off the dispersal.) The light faded quickly as dusk fell.

It was a tremendous relief to climb aboard at last and to be doing something, although even at this late hour it was possible for the Op to be "scrubbed" – some crews got as far as waiting to take off at the end of the runway only to learn that their mission had been cancelled. The aircrew donned their parachute harnesses as the ground crew brought up the trolley accumulators. These were banks of batteries to power the starter motor of each Merlin engine. "Don't bring 'em back, boys!" was a frequent farewell wisecrack from the ground crew, referring to the bombs.

The seven men climbed up the ladder into the darkness of the bomber's fuselage. The rear-gunner made his way down the narrowing fuselage towards the tail, sliding over the raised tailplane spar, passing through the bulkhead doors (which were then closed after him by another crew member). He hung his parachute with elastic hooks onto the fuselage wall before dropping down into his turret and, once seated, reached around behind him to close the turret's sliding doors. The Fraser Nash turrets were very compact and could not accommodate both a gunner and his parachute. "It wasn't a job for a big fella," explains Jimmy James, a former rear gunner.

Now sealed off from the rest of the crew (and his parachute) his only means of communication was via the intercom and, should he need to bale out, he had to open the sliding doors (assuming his turret could be turned to the correct position to allow this), retrieve and clip on his parachute, rotate the turret 90 degrees and fall out backwards into the night sky. This was hardly an easy matter in a wildly spinning aircraft, or with flames roaring down the fuselage.

Meanwhile, the bomb-aimer, pilot, flight engineer, navigator, wireless operator and mid-upper gunner had taken their positions further forwards. The pilot had a raised seat with arm rests. His parachute was attached to him permanently (as the last to leave the aircraft in an emergency, he needed to have it on him for a rapid exit), and he sat on it so it doubled as a seat cushion. He had an armour-plated bulkhead behind him, the only crew member to have any protection, although it would not have been much help against a 20mm cannon shell from a German fighter. Directly behind the pilot and at right angles, facing the port side of the fuselage, sat the navigator who had a desk with an angle-poise lamp, his maps spread out before him. Behind him, but facing forwards, was the wireless operator. Further back down the fuselage and suspended by a harness in his turret was the mid-upper gunner. The occupants of the cockpit had a clear view back along the top of the fuselage to the mid-upper gunner from the raised astrodome (used for taking starshots to assist with navigation and also for observation).

The crew plugged their masks into the intercom sockets by their seats and the pilot checked everyone was in contact with one another. There was a microphone in each oxygen mask and headphones in the flying helmets. After many hours wearing the masks, some men found their faces uncomfortably chaffed (American crews had throat microphones, but they were not as clear). By now, the evening silence was being shattered as engines could be heard starting up intermittently around the airfield and shadowy forms of bombers could be seen beginning to move in the gloom.

The Lancaster's engines were started one by one in a set sequence and the sound was deafening. The aircraft shuddered uncomfortably until all four were running, when it became rhythmic and reassuring. Jim Flint recalls that he didn't need to look at his dials to see if the engines were all right: he was a keen lover of music and he could tell when all four were running in harmony. "It was like listening to a church organ," he explains. "A really beautiful sound."

With the aircraft now alive, the pilot and flight engineer carried out final checks. The tension rose with each passing minute and Ron Mather, sitting in his wireless operator's seat, remembers being shot at by a nervous rear-gunner in another Lancaster. "He let rip," says Ron. "We were shot up before we'd even left the ground!" He spent the entire mission with the wind whistling through the holes in the roof of the fuselage above his head, thankful that he had been sitting down at the time.

At a signal from the flight engineer, the wooden chocks were pulled away by the ground crew and, with a burst of power to get her moving, the Lancaster rolled forward, eager to take up her allotted position in the queue of bombers trundling along the perimeter from their dispersals, making for the duty runway. The perimeter track was narrow and winding, and aircraft might have to travel more than a mile to the marshalling point at the end of the runway. The pilot was supposed to taxi the Lancaster at fast walking pace – not easy to judge from his seat nearly twenty feet above the ground – and he kept a grip of the brake lever at all times.

Having reached the marshalling point, the pilot and flight engineer did final system checks including trim, mixture, fuel and flaps. The rear gunner quietly double-checked that his turret was facing dead astern. The Lancaster in front of them roared off down the runway, and a flash of green light from the caravan at the far end indicated to the next crew that it had taken off safely and that it was their turn to move onto the runway and line up.

The pilot and flight engineer increased the revs to half-power to ensure all four engines were running smoothly and to keep the plugs clean. The noise increased as the Lancaster began to strain impatiently against her brakes. Finally released, she surged forward, gathering speed, the pilot keeping his eye on the centre line of the runway and listening to the airspeed being called out by the navigator every few seconds to aid him. The flight engineer placed his hand behind the pilot's and as the throttles were pushed forwards to three-quarters open, the pilot removed his hand and the engineer took over, continuing to push the throttles through the "gate" to reach a tremendous 3,000 rpm.

The Lancaster had a well-known tendency to pull strongly to port on take off; to counter this, power from the port engines was increased to keep her straight. Her speed was now 90 knots (104 mph). Racing along the runway, her tail came up and she suddenly became streamlined and elegant. With the tail raised, the rudder could now be used to help offset the pull to port.

For the crew, these moments as they hurtled towards the end of the runway were hazardous; a burst tyre at this point would spell disaster with 2,000 gallons of high octane fuel and a full bomb load around them.

A small knot of well-wishing WAAFs and ground crew would wave to the Lancaster as it tore past; the rear-gunner acknowledged them and waved back. "We were too young to be frightened," said Jimmy. "We never actually thought we would get the chop". The Lancaster had reached 110 knots (127 mph) by now and moments later a sinking sensation and a sudden absence of vibration indicated to the crew that the she was airborne. The wheels now retracted and her speed gradually increased to 155 knots (178 mph). As the Lancasters thundered over the River Trent and passed close to Hoveringham, young Eileen Lawton came outside The Old Elm Tree pub to wave a tea-towel. The bombers were so low that very often the rear-gunner waved back. "They were our friends," she remembers. "They were such nice young men." One resident in Hoveringham describes the Lancasters taking off: "One after another, passing across the face of the full moon, just visible behind the walnut trees in the grounds of Hoveringham Hall". Flying towards Nottingham, the heavily-laden aircraft steadily gained height before finally banking and changing direction for the continent

By the time the WAAFs, ground crew and other well-wishers huddled by the side of the runway had made their way back to the warmth of the airfield buildings, the first of the bombers and their crews were nearly a hundred miles away, heading east and climbing. The bomber stream had reached 10,000 feet when they crossed the English coast and would attain their cruising altitude of 20,000 feet before entering enemy territory. The aircrafts' navigational lights were extinguished at this point.

Facing backwards in his lonely eyrie, the rear-gunner contemplated the last threads of the setting sun in the west behind them (and no doubt wondered if he would live to see it rise again). As the bomber climbed, he was increasingly aware of the mercury tumbling, as sub-zero temperatures and a vicious gale roared in through the open panel in his gun turret. (Sitting in the slip-stream of an aircraft travelling at around 200 mph was noisy, and many rear-gunners blame that exposure for the hearing-aids they now wear.) His bulky electrically-heated suit and gloves had been plugged in before take-off, tingling as they heated up, which helped counter the cold (it could get down to –40°C) but there were hazards even with these. If the fabric on the gloves became worn from use, the heating wires were exposed and could give the gunner a nasty shock when he gripped the guns. Some men sweated in their suits and short-circuits and burns were not unknown.

The crew were all engaged with their individual tasks. The pilot was constantly checking the repeater compass, air speed indicator, horizon and moon in that order. Generally he flew with his left hand and reset instruments with his right, although both hands were needed for flying once over enemy territory.

The navigator, curtained off from the cockpit to contain the light from his angle-poise lamp, was constantly checking the course and air speed, grateful to be fully occupied as they reached enemy territory all too soon. Calculating the true air speed was enough to occupy anyone's mind: the indicated air speed might be 170 knots (196 mph), but the true air speed could be as much as 240 knots (276 mph). In addition, he was kept busy using navigational aids such as "Gee" (and later the even more accurate "H2S") to plot their position on his maps and ensure they were on the correct course. There was no room for error in navigation. If you strayed off the designated flight path, you had little fuel to spare to allow for corrections. One navigator had been an architect before joining the RAF, and the lines he drew on his maps during operations were so unbelievably precise and neat that the maps were kept by the Air Ministry as examples to future students. Douglas Hudson, another navigator, found his note book was black and barely legible from the graphite on his hands: he had been handling "Window", the graphite-covered strips of foil pushed out of bombers by crews to deceive German radar.

The flight engineer was responsible for the undercarriage, flaps, throttles and propellers. He had to be capable of flying the aircraft in an emergency: most engineers could manage a straight line but anything more demanding would have been beyond their rudimentary piloting skills. He was also in charge of checking and maintaining the fuel levels. It was crucial that the six fuel tanks were kept as evenly balanced as possible and he would change the tank in use every twenty minutes or so to prevent any one becoming empty (perversely, empty tanks, being full of vapour, exploded more readily than full ones and the risk to tanks from flak and fighter shells was all too present). The only light in the cockpit was from the glow of the instruments and he used a shaded torch to check his jotted calculations. When not monitoring the dials and instruments, he kept his eyes peeled for the tell-tale four glows which betrayed the exhausts of other Lancasters in front and above. With no navigation lights, collision was a very real risk with evasive action often required immediately to avoid calamity. Roy Mather, a wireless operator, recalls there being barely twenty yards between his bomber's wing-tip and that of the bomber flying alongside.

The bomber continued towards its destination and searchlights were now visible ahead, sweeping high into the skies to seek out the bombers. The master searchlight was radar-controlled and, when it had fixed on a bomber, the anti-aircraft guns, known as "flak", could then focus their deadly firepower on it. Within moments, other beams swivelled to join the direction of the master searchlight. For a bomber which found itself "coned" by several of these intense bluish blinding beams, the only escape was to undertake violent evasive manoeuvres. Apart from the sheer horror of being blinded at great speed, the crew was fully aware that, unless they escaped the beams' snare, they were sitting ducks for the flak which would come within seconds and try to blow them out of the sky.

Flak could reach well over 20,000 feet and was greatly feared. The mighty German flak defences stretched from the sea to Berlin and beyond. To the crews, it looked as though they were flying through a horizontal cloud of hundreds of puffs of smoke. But the "puffs" were deadly: each one was an exploding anti-aircraft shell, and those close to aircraft were seen by the crew as bright flashes. Flak shells were fired by heavy guns at a rate of two a minute. The red-hot shrapnel from flak could penetrate aircraft and men and cause terrible damage. The sound of fragments hitting the bomber has been likened to heavy hail on a tin roof. Flak left gaping holes in aircraft and yet, somehow, many made it home with daylight visible through their wings and tails, pieces of alloy skin trailing forlornly behind.

A bomber unlucky enough to be hit directly by flak, or in a vulnerable spot such as its bomb load or fuel tanks, was doomed. Exploding bombers were clearly visible to other crews as "very bright flashes" in the darkness. Predictive flak was radar-controlled, the shells getting closer with each burst to the bomber. Unless it began drastic action to escape, it would be caught. One rear-gunner who saw Lancasters pursued by this flak, described the sequence as "flash, flash, flash...bang" as the lethal explosions homed in on a bomber before succeeding in destroying it. The flak guns then moved on to the next bomber.

Below the crews was a ghastly panorama of fire and explosions on the ground. Bombers had to fly straight and level for at least a whole minute prior to dropping their bombs, whilst the bomb-aimer checked the target indicators on the ground and guided his pilot to the exact release point. This was the crew's most vulnerable time, and the seconds until the bomb-aimer finally announced "Bombs gone" seemed endless. The risk of bombs dropping from Lancasters above them in the stream was also significant, and the wireless operator was put to use as an extra lookout in the astrodome to warn his pilot of this danger.

With the bombs dropped and the photo flash of the target gone off, the crew could turn away with relief and set a course for home, desperate to escape the boiling cauldron of hell all around them.

Meanwhile, the enemy had been alerted to their presence and knew their likely route back to England. Fighters would have been mobilised and were now waiting for the returning bombers. Roy Hill's Lancaster was attacked by a German night fighter, and the first he knew of it as he sat at his wireless operator's table was a deafening crash as shells tore mercilessly through the fuselage, killing the mid-upper gunner who was left suspended in his harness, beyond all help. The rear-gunner was also killed. Fighters almost always attacked bombers from the rear or, later in the war, from underneath using upward-firing cannons. Attacking out of the bright moon was another tactic they had perfected. The rear-gunner was therefore the eyes in the back of the head for the entire crew, anxiously rotating his turret as he scanned the darkness for danger. He was expressly told at gunnery school not to be tempted to look down at the exploding bombs on the ground, for fear of spoiling his night vision. Some gunners managed to fire back at fighters as they struck, and several were confirmed as shot down by Lancasters. The smell of cordite in the fuselage from the Lancaster's guns as they fired was overpowering. One harrowing account from another crew described a blazing Lancaster being attacked repeatedly by a fighter. Five parachutes were seen to open but the rear-gunner was obviously trapped in his turret and continued to fire. The fighter went back for another blast with the gunner still defiantly firing away, when the Lancaster blew up. "I have never seen such bravery," said the eyewitness. "Poor bugger".

A bomber crew needed to escape a fighter as quickly as possible, following instructions from the rear gunner to the pilot about the appropriate direction to flee in order to spoil the fighter pilot's aim. The ensuing "corkscrew" manoeuvre has passed into history for sheer awfulness, but it was the most successful escape tactic and was practised ruthlessly by trainee bomber crews: it saved many lives. To be in an aircraft as it writhed and twisted frantically across the sky in an attempt to escape a fighter, especially when the bomber was fully laden with bombs, was "no fun at all," explains a former flight engineer. The pilot was the only member of the crew to have a harness and was anchored to his controls (although the flight engineer had a rudimentary lap-strap), but the rest of the crew had to cling on for dear life to avoid being flung all over the aircraft. As it corkscrewed, it simultaneously lost a drastic amount of height and anything unsecured in the bomber was likewise re-arranged around the fuselage. The rear gunner, floating helplessly and pinned by g-force to the roof of his turret, was only held in place by his flying boots which were wedged under the gun mechanism. Loose .303 shells flew everywhere around him. One navigator narrowly missed injury when his dividers flew up, then came down and embedded themselves in his table inches from his hand. Douglas Hudson's Lancaster corkscrewed non-stop from 19,000 to 9,000 feet and he was truly terrified. It took the combined strength of three men – the pilot, Douglas (who was the navigator) and the nineteen-year-old flight engineer – to haul on the control column and to level out before the bomber lost any more height. Once they had shaken off the fighter, they began their laborious ascent back to rejoin the bomber stream – all of which used up more valuable fuel.

Having negotiated the German defences for the second time that night, those bomber crews crossing the Channel almost dared to hope that they would be back to enjoy their eggs and bacon. They consumed thermos flasks of coffee, as well as orange juice, chocolate and sweets (all too frequently devoured before the target was even reached!). Ron Mather's pilot asked him, as wireless operator, to switch on the wireless and see what music was playing. It was very early one Sunday morning and the morning church service was being broadcast. The strains of "Nearer my God to Thee" could be discerned, at which point the pilot decided the hymn might be tempting fate and ordered the thing to be turned off at once!

But for many crews, ruptured fuel tanks, damaged engines, severe damage to the fabric of the aircraft making it unstable, as well as injured crew members, added to the anxiety of the final miles. Jane Gates, living directly under the route the Lancasters took over Hoveringham to reach the runway at Syerston, said that the stricken engines made the returning bombers coming over their roofs sound as though they had the hiccoughs. Another villager said that the Lancasters "took off in bulk cash and returned in penny numbers, from all directions". When Ron Mather was returning from a raid on Munich to Fulbeck near Newark, his Lancaster was in the circuit to land when, to the crew's horror, the aircraft in front was shot down by one of two German fighters which had simply followed the bombers back to England, unnoticed by the weary airmen. The Lancaster behind them was also badly damaged by the fighters.

Tired crews were frequently greeted by the dreaded winter fog over their airfield, and many young men survived the horror of a raid to Germany, only to die in crashes caused by poor visibility on their return to England. Fatigue was inevitable after a raid which could last up to ten hours and with the adrenalin gone, a chasm remained which exhaustion soon filled. Ron Mather recalled being in a Lancaster approaching Syerston after a lengthy flight. As the bomber passed over the Hoveringham pastures and neared the River Trent, Ron heard the flight engineer suddenly shout to the pilot in alarm. Seconds later the Lancaster accelerated with maximum power and climbed sharply, just clearing the ground at the end of the runway. The pilot circuited the airfield before finally coming in to land safely. It transpired the Lancaster had been about 100 feet below the height of the runway (which, as described in Chapter Seven, is 150 feet above the river) and the aircraft had been heading for oblivion on the wooded hillside. Exhaustion affected everyone's judgment on occasion.

Once safely landed, the crews were picked up by trucks and transported to the station buildings for debriefing by Intelligence officers, a cup of tea and a cigarette. The images of the target recorded by each aircraft's photo flash were taken away to be scrutinised by Intelligence. Breakfast followed, with the men trying not to dwell on the empty spaces left by missing crews who had been present only a few hours before at the previous evening's meal. Finally, the crews were free head for their beds, just as the rest of the airfield was awakening for another day.

This was the life that the young crews of Lancasters JB125 and LM308 had trained for and were impatient to take part in. Fate, fickle as ever, was to dictate otherwise on two freezing January nights in 1945.

Chapter Nine

"SUCH NICE YOUNG MEN..."

The Crew of Lancaster MkIII JB125
Crashed 2150hrs Friday 12 January 1945, Hoveringham

This crew should have completed their training at Syerston by this time and already been posted to an operational squadron. However, the winter weather was so appalling that many flights were "scrubbed" (according to the navigator, Peter Hill's last letter home in January) and the crew was frustrated to see their training schedule disrupted and delayed.

Guy Dunlop, the pilot, and his crew had completed a three-hour cross-country night flight and had returned to the sky above RAF Syerston to await instructions. Dunlop was instructed to rejoin the circuit at 2121hrs. Shortly afterwards, at 2142hrs, he called the airfield and was given a time to land, which he did not acknowledge. At 2148hrs, Dunlop called a second time and was again given a time to land, but replied that he was at 1,000 feet and could not see the ground. There was persistent drizzle beneath the cloud base (recorded as 500–600 feet) and a north easterly wind of 30 mph. Dunlop was instructed to descend to 700 feet, which he acknowledged, and, at this point, the Airfield Controller saw him break cloud downwind momentarily and turn in a tight circle. Dunlop radioed to say that he could see the "funnel" (the approach to the airfield) and seemed to approach the airfield flying down the funnel, before disappearing into cloud again. A few seconds later, the Airfield Controller watched the Lancaster "banking violently" to port over the funnel, at a height only just above that of the airfield. Despite the Lancaster's starboard navigation light being almost vertically above the port, Dunlop seemed satisfied that he had control of the aircraft, saying, "Over Funnel" moments before the Airfield Controller saw his aircraft plunge to the ground.

JB125 had roared over the Hall side of the village and narrowly missed the Women's Land Army hostel on Lodgefield Lane. Margaret Rigley was billeted there at the time and recalls the girls, who were not yet in bed, being petrified by the noise of the low-flying aircraft and thinking they were about to lose their roof. Moments later they heard a loud "whoomph" and rushed upstairs from where they could see a "huge fire" in a nearby field.

The Lancaster had come down in the riverside pasture near the Old Elm Tree pub. From marks on the ground, the accident investigators later concluded that the first part of the aircraft to strike the ground had been the port outer airscrew. The starboard wing missed one of the 12-foot high anti-enemy poles dotted around the field. The pole was sited five yards from the airscrew's point of impact, which confirmed that the aircraft had been banking to port when it struck the ground. It travelled along the grass field on its belly, through a hedge and into the next field, missing a shed containing a tractor (the shed and tractor are still in working condition in Hoveringham) before coming to rest a few yards further on and blowing up. Many villagers raced to help, but the crew had already perished in the inferno.

The Court of Inquiry concluded that, although the weather conditions would have presented little difficulty for an experienced pilot, Dunlop, who had only four hours solo night-flying experience, should have been diverted to another airfield by Control at RAF Syerston. Following this accident, instructions were issued that, when the cloud base was below 1,000 feet or visibility less than 2,000 yards, no aircraft was to be landed at Syerston without prior reference to the Station Commander or Chief Instructor.

The men who died in that Lancaster were:

Guy Rerenui Dunlop
Pilot

Guy was born in March 1916 in Wanganui, New Zealand. His grandparents had originally travelled to New Zealand from Ayrshire, Scotland in 1855. He enjoyed a carefree childhood near the Wanganui River, with his two brothers and three sisters. After school, he attended Massey Agricultural College and obtained a Diploma of Agriculture. His interests were rugby, hunting and tennis. He was employed in farming when he enlisted in the RNZAF in 1942. The following year he was posted to the Elementary Flying School at Harewood, and in May 1943 he embarked for Alberta, Canada. At Flying Training School there he learned to fly Avro Ansons, before leaving for England in October. A spell flying Oxfords at Croughton, Northamptonshire, followed and, in June 1944, he went to the Operational Training Unit (OTU) at

Abingdon, Oxfordshire, where he met his crew. Guy was promoted to Pilot Officer in August 1944. In September, he transferred to 1669 Conversion Unit at Langar, Nottinghamshire (only a few miles from RAF Syerston) where he converted to Halifaxes and finally, on 20 November, he moved with his crew to No. 5 LFS at RAF Syerston. Despite the dreadful cold weather in January 1945, Guy generously donated his clothing coupons to his young navigator, Peter Hill, who did not have any gloves.

After Guy's death, his trunk was returned to his parents at Matamata. A Christmas card which Guy posted to his family on 23 December 1944 was received two weeks after he was killed. In it, he thanked his brother for asking him to be godfather to his nephew and agreed with pleasure to undertake this responsibility. Guy's memory lives on through many of his male relatives named after him (including his nephew, Guy "Rollo" Dunlop).

Guy was buried with full service honours at Oxford Botley Cemetery. He had amassed 451 hours as a pilot.

Peter John Hill
Navigator

Peter was born on 26 August 1922 in Picton, New Zealand. His parents moved soon after this to Spring Creek, Marlborough. Peter's father was a First World War veteran (he had been wounded in his leg during that war and suffered pain from it all his life), and was a respected accountant and member of his local community. Peter attended Marlborough College and his interests were swimming, tennis, football, cricket and running. He was employed as a clerk by Dalgety & Co., Blenheim, and also served in the Territorials before he enlisted in May 1942. His elder brother, Howard, had been killed in the Battle of Britain on 20 September 1940 and Peter, hoping to follow Howard as a pilot, was bitterly disappointed when his flying training was terminated by the Air Force and he was re-mustered to Air Observer. After recovering from a bout of illness, he embarked for Canada in August 1943 where he was posted to No. 7 Air Observers' School, Manitoba. He qualified as a navigator in February 1944 and arrived in England in April that year. A brief spell on bleak Anglesey followed, and then in June he was sent to Abingdon to train on Avro Ansons and Whitleys. Here he became good friends with Albert Evans, the bomb-aimer in his newly-formed crew. In October he was posted to 1669 CU at Langar to fly Halifaxes, and in December he was sent to No. 5 LFS, Syerston to convert to Lancasters.

Peter is buried at Oxford Botley Cemetery. He had accumulated 273 hours as a navigator.

His father treasured the photograph of his two young sons playing by the sea until his death. It always reminded him of how both boys had loved adventure and freedom.

Albert John Evans BEM
Bomb Aimer

Albert was born in Treorchy, South Wales in 1919. Known universally as Jack, he joined the Glamorgan Constabulary in February 1938. On 29 April 1941, a nearby mining village called Cwmparc was bombed by the Luftwaffe, when incendiaries and then high explosive bombs were dropped. 27 men, women and children were killed, including three evacuee children from the same family from London (they were buried together in a single grave). Albert worked throughout the night, rescuing a woman and child from "mountains of debris" from Treharne Street, where most of the bombs had fallen. At one point a bomb exploded only fifteen yards from where he was digging through burning rubble. Albert's wife recalled that when he finally returned home, he was so exhausted that he fell asleep with his eyes open. The Home Secretary, Herbert Morrison (by coincidence the son of a police constable), was so impressed by Albert's gallant conduct under "extremely difficult and dangerous conditions" that he was awarded the British Empire Medal, Civil Division. He joined the RAF in 1942 and spent time in Canada, training to be a bomb-aimer. He returned to England and at the OTU in Abingdon, he struck up a close friendship with Peter Hill, his navigator. Peter refers to Albert as "Taff" in his diary and mentions that it was difficult to accompany Albert to his home during leave, as he was married. (Albert's son, John, was born in March 1945, two months after Albert's death.)

Albert is buried at Oxford Botley Cemetery.

Richard Ludgvan Staples
Wireless Operator/Air Gunner

Richard was born on 26 April 1921 in Edinburgh. His family moved to New Zealand but, in 1925 when Richard was four years old, his mother was killed by a horse. His father left his children (Richard, Harry, Bert and Jean) in the care of the Salvation Army at Masterton and headed to Australia to work. He wrote a letter to his children explaining why he was moving to Australia, but they were too young to comprehend his letter, which was put in one of their apron pockets and went through the wash before any adults could see it and read it to them. Their father died in Australia two years later and the children became orphans. The Salvation Army waived the rules to accommodate Harry, who was technically too young to stay in the Home, so that the children could remain together. Jean was particularly close to her brother Richard and, after he died, his Air Force photo was prominently displayed in her home. The family remembers how Richard, whom they called Dick, would "light up any room". He grew into a stocky lad, and was employed as a farm worker in Carterton when he joined up in October 1942, thrilled to have the chance of service. He spent his first night in the RNZAF sleeping on the bare grandstand boards in the Solway Showgrounds, Masterton, with other recruits; not surprisingly, he described this as "uncomfortable". His record describes him as having an "inferiority complex", but being a "very nice lad". He was left-handed and "not lacking in courage". After completing his wireless operator course at Rotorua, he went to Calgary, Canada, in April 1943. He was awarded his wireless operator/air gunner badge at Mossbank, Saskatchewan, and promoted to sergeant, then flight sergeant. Richard arrived in Brighton, England in February 1944, and was posted to the Observer Advanced Flying Unit at West Freugh airfield, Wigtownshire, in May. The following month saw him sent to Abingdon where he trained on Whitleys and met the rest of his crew. In October, he and his new crew transferred to 1669 CU Langar to convert to Halifaxes, and on 3 December he arrived with them at No. 5 LFS, RAF Syerston.

Richard was buried at Oxford Botley Cemetery. The coffin was covered with the Union Jack and the "Last Post" was played. He had accrued 215 hours as a wireless operator/air gunner.

Patrick Joseph Vincent Browne
Flight Engineer

Patrick was born into a devout Catholic family in Barking, Essex, the youngest of five children. He was an "altar server" at his church, St. Mary and St. Ethelburga, Barking, along with his best friend, Pat Bearfield. Patrick was also a member of Barking Catholic Club and a neighbour described him as a "quiet, clean-cut young man with a ready smile and soft voice. He was very good company". His brother-in-law, Albert Jenkins, remembers him as "quiet, but with a great sense of humour". Patrick was an apprentice toolmaker at the Gaslighting Coke Company in Beckton. His elder brother, Vincent, was in the Home Guard and was also employed at the same gasworks. (Vincent was killed, ten days before the birth of his daughter Pauline, when he was hit by a bus as he rode his motorbike to work one foggy morning in 1941.) Patrick enjoyed making balsa models of aircraft and there were dozens of them pinned to his bedroom ceiling. He had always been keen on aircraft and shared this interest with Pat Bearfield, who was in the ATC. He joined up when he was eighteen, saying he was worried the war would be over before he was involved in it. He was an excellent dancer and much preferred the social scene in Newark to that in Nottingham.

Patrick was killed three weeks before his sister Celia's wedding, at which he was due to be Best Man. The family received the telegram informing them of his death on Saturday 13 January. His father sat unmoving in a chair for two days, utterly distraught. Two days later, on Monday, they received his last letter to them, which he had posted on Friday evening, just a few hours before he was killed. Patrick had half-finished a balsa model of a Lancaster, which his cousin Michael Kelly treasured for many years (it was never finished).

Patrick was buried in Rippleside Cemetery, Barking, in the same plot as both his older brother, Vincent, and Vincent's wife, Winifred.

Richard Henry Sedgley
Rear Gunner

Born in the beautiful Cotswold village of Upper Oddington, Richard was one of ten children and was known by everyone as Dick. The family lived at Sedgley Cottage (there had been Sedgleys in Oddington for many generations). Their father was the gardener at the "big house", Oddington Top, owned by Colonel Martin, and their mother took in laundry from local families, including the Martins. She had a beautiful voice and sang as she hung the laundry out in their orchard. Dick attended the village school and joined the North Cotswold ATC when he was seventeen, in May 1941. He worked at Mr. Cox's farm in Oddington, milking cows and doing other chores. Popular with the villagers, he was a "handsome chap" according to his sister, Phyllis, as well as a regular church-goer.

The family was no stranger to tragedy: Dick's brother, Claude, had been in the army and was killed when his troopship was blown up in the Mediterranean, and his sister, Kath, died of an unidentified illness aged 21 during the war.

Dick's coffin was met at Adlestrop station on Tuesday 16 January by his father, who accompanied it for the short journey home to

Oddington. The funeral procession was watched from the school windows by Dick's younger sisters, Phyllis and Maggie, who were considered too young to attend the funeral. Dick was buried at Oddington (St. Nicholas) church, which stands alone half a mile from the village at the end of a quiet country lane. Maggie believes that her mother was always singing because it helped her cope with the distress of losing her children. The family received many letters from people in the RAF Syerston area who knew and liked Dick.

His sister Phyllis, now seventy-seven, still visits the same farm where her brother Dick was employed over sixty-five years ago.

William Fordyce Cairns
Air Gunner

Sadly, I have been unable to find any trace of William's family in Glasgow. His parents were Hector MacDonald Cairns and Elizabeth Fordyce Cairns, of Mosspark, Glasgow. Hector was a Trade Union Legal Representative. William is buried in Glasgow Cardonald Cemetery. He was 19 years old.

The Crew of Lancaster LM308
Crashed 0216hrs Monday 29 January 1945, Hoveringham

Pilot Richard Rathbone and his crew took off at one minute past midnight to complete "Exercise 7", a night cross-country sortie or "Moon Training Flight", followed by practice bombing exercise.

Cloud base was over 3,000 feet, with no icing reported, and there was a light northerly wind. Visibility was good. They returned to base and Rathbone called up on the R/T for permission to carry out practice bombing. This was refused, as the bombing range was covered by cloud, and at 0214hrs he was told to rejoin the circuit, which he acknowledged. He gave no indication of his aircraft being unserviceable. At 0215hrs, two eyewitnesses reported seeing the aircraft diving at great speed and in flames, followed by an explosion heard by many people at the airfield and nearby villages. Bill Halley, the rear-gunner, was ill that night (his replacement was Jasper Martin) but watched his friends take off; the mid-upper gunner Joe FitzGibbon was his childhood friend. After the accident, he wrote in a letter to the FitzGibbon family: "About one or two in the morning, the boys heard a loud noise." He continued: "They were seen over base, trying to land. Their port engines were on fire, the next they just blew up, nobody got out." It was the first time Halley had been grounded and he finished: "At present I am looking for a new crew but I shall never get another crew as the boys [sic]".

The official report states that LM308 "crashed at high speed and exploded on impact". The cause of the accident remains obscure, although the Court of Inquiry agreed that the aircraft had got out of control and Rathbone had been unable to regain control before hitting the ground. Because the wreckage was so widely dispersed after the explosion, it was impossible to ascertain the cause of the crash.

The unfortunate Land Army Girls in their hostel witnessed this crash too. On this occasion, Margaret Rigley remembers that they were awoken by a "tremendous bang", and, as the girls looked out of their windows, they couldn't believe that they were seeing flames in virtually the same spot as the Lancaster which had crashed seventeen days earlier. She and her friend June went to see the crash site in the morning, where it was guarded by two RAF soldiers. The debris was spread over many fields and was unrecognisable as ever having been a plane. She remembers seeing half a pound note, perfect apart from its burnt edges, before she and June left the scene in distress. It was an "appalling sight," she says. This crash happened at the end of a week of intense cold, severe frosts and icy roads, already described in the summary about JB125's crew, who, of course, were experiencing the same weather conditions. Rathbone mentions in his last letter home, written the day before he was killed, that "we've been standing by night after night to fly, but the weather's been bad and it's so late by the time they scrub it that all you can do is go to the camp cinema". On 25 January, the crew "walked and after standing on a river bank for about 15 minutes whistling and yelling a fellow came across in a boat to an old pub where we spent the night" (this was the Old Elm Tree pub in Hoveringham). It was "the first time in seven weeks we've been able to sleep in". He also writes: "it's been so cold lately that it's not much fun going out". The crew's last training flight was meant to be on 27 January but seems to have been postponed, most likely because of the weather, until 28 January, when their Lancaster crashed.

The night of 29/30 January, twenty-four hours after the crash, seven inches of snow fell, according to the Hoveringham School log (half the children failed to attend school on 30 January) which seems to have hindered recovery of the crash, as pieces were being found up to a year later by local farmers.

The men who died in this Lancaster were:

Richard Barlow Rathbone
Pilot

Richard was born on 20 September 1916 in Hamilton, Ontario. He left school aged sixteen and attended the Canada Business College, where his character was noted as being "...of highest degree". His family remembers him as very much the dare-devil compared to his younger brother Arthur, and his interests included hunting, skiing, hockey and baseball. Richard was also a very accomplished artist. He enrolled in the RCAF in 1942, having been an office clerk at the Brown Wire Speciality Company for eight years. He began his flying training on Tiger Moths and Harvards in 1943. After flying Wellingtons at an OTU in northern Scotland, he met his crew in July, had a final eye check in September 1944, and was posted to 1669 CU at Langar in November to convert to Halifaxes with his newly formed crew. His rear-gunner, Bill Halley (who survived the war – see below) remembers that Richard was nicknamed "Pappy" by his crew because, at 28, he was quite a bit older than them. During his time at Langar, Richard had to make an emergency landing in Tangmere when two of the four engines on his Halifax failed at 18,000 feet and "shook the plane about so that we hardly knew what was happening," according to a letter Richard wrote to his mother. He described how he ordered his crew to take up their crash positions and that he "didn't think he was nervous". It was described by other air force personnel as a skilful landing under very difficult circumstances. Richard and his crew were picked up from Tangmere and returned to Langar in a Lancaster, about which he wrote: "...by its performance, I think I shall like them". From Langar, Richard and his crew was posted to No. 5 LFS at RAF Syerston to complete their training, flying Lancasters.

He is buried in Stonefall Cemetery, Harrogate.

Hugh Munro MacKenzie
Navigator

Born on 30 March 1923 in Portmahomack, Scotland, Hugh was the youngest of five children – the "baby of the family" according to his niece. His father, Farquhar, had joined the British Army at fourteen and had served in the Seaforth Highlanders, seeing action in the Boer War and in India. The family moved to Toronto where Farquhar became a bank messenger. Hugh was a talented footballer and was known for his infectious and mischievous sense of humour. Before joining up he worked for the United Steel Corporation in Toronto as an office clerk. The last time many of his family saw him was Christmas Eve 1942, when Hugh was best man at his brother Simon's wedding to Laura. The RAF report described him as "keen and hardworking". He didn't drink or smoke, but his fellow crew members "didn't hold that against him!" according to Bill Halley (again, see below), who remembers Hugh clearly. After being awarded his Navigator's badge on 23 December 1943, Hugh was posted to 20 OTU Abingdon in June 1944, where he met his crew, and was promoted to Flight Sergeant in September. A move to 1669 CU at Langar followed the same month, with a final transfer to No. 5 LFS at RAF Syerston on 17 December 1944.

Hugh's sister, Margaret, adored her brother and painted his portrait. Hugh's older brother Donald missed him terribly, and, after Hugh's death, would read Hugh's log book to feel a connection to his lost brother. Hugh's mother saw her three oldest sons return safely from the war, but the loss of her beloved youngest child meant that she was "never the same again".

Hugh was buried at 10.30am on Friday 2 February 1945 in Harrogate Stonefall Cemetery.

John Alexander Emerson
Air Bomber

John was born in Vancouver on 22 November 1914. His father had been born in Iceland and had moved to Canada as a child. John's mother, who was English, died before he joined the RCAF. John had two sisters and was keen on basketball, bowling, tennis and skating; he was nervous around dogs having been bitten on the face as a small child (he had scarring on his right cheek as an adult). A practical man, his skills included electrical wiring, plumbing and carpentry and he was employed as a "motorman" and also a trolley bus operator in Vancouver, before enlisting in September 1942. However, he appears to have been fairly accident-prone, particularly during rugby games, suffering repeated injuries to his knees and ankles. At Air Observer School, where he flew Avro Ansons, he was described as "carefree with ability" but "careless in dress" and a "garrulous fellow"! He was also on record as "an excellent Air Bomber", who could have been an "average pilot" but who wished to be a navigator. He embarked for England in November 1943, leaving his wife Phyllis behind in their home at Hollyburn, BC. John was promoted to Flight Sergeant in August 1944, before transferring with his crew to 1669 CU at Langar on 20 October. After his thirtieth birthday (he was older than most airmen) he was posted to No. 5 LFS at RAF Syerston.

After his death, his widow received his brown suitcase with his personal effects, but noticed that several personal items which had been anniversary presents from her to John were missing. The Director of Estates wrote to Phyllis to explain as kindly as he could that these items had probably been on his person at the time of the crash, and lost forever, but the whole saga only added to her distress.

John Henry Reid
Wireless Operator/Air Gunner

John was born on 12 May 1924 in Stanley, New Brunswick. A sporty lad called Jack by everyone, he was a member of the basketball team which became New Brunswick champions in 1941. He was also a good catcher in baseball. He attended Fredericton High School, where he met Glaidus and, aged sixteen, they started going out together. The High School's 700 pupils had raised $2,500 for victims of air raids in Britain (the local families listened to daily news reports on the war overseas), many of the young men impatient to graduate and begin military training to help the war effort. John left school in 1942 and his church minister described him as a boy with "an upright character and straightforward sincerity". John and Glaidus married in January 1943 and had a baby girl, Lorna. After completing his training as a wireless operator/air gunner, John embarked for England in early 1944, was posted with his crew to 1669 CU at Langar and finally transferred to No. 5 LFS RAF Syerston on 17 December. His record states that he was "keen and conscientious, with an exemplary manner and bearing".

On 30 January 1945, Glaidus was working at the Marysville Cotton Mill, and wondered why her boss kept going past her door and looking in at her. It transpired he had just been informed of John's death and hadn't the heart to tell her. Her family came to the mill and broke the news to her instead.

John is buried in Harrogate Stonefall Cemetery. His widow, Glaidus, is a leading member of her local Legion and on many occasions has laid the wreath at Remembrance Services on 11 November.

Joseph Francis FitzGibbon
Mid-Upper Gunner

One of nine children, Joe was born in St. John's, Newfoundland, on 6 April 1924. The family lived on Hamilton Avenue, St. John's, and spent many summers in Placentia, the birth place of Joe's mother, Pauline Kemp. Joe's father (also called Joe) had a colourful career in Newfoundland politics. Young Joe was a "quiet lad", who was a noted speaker in school debates and keen on woodwork and hockey. He was well remembered as being a "gentlemanly figure". He left St. Bonaventure's College, St. John's, with merit, and worked for a while as an office boy, before moving to the Ministry of Public Works "to better myself" according to his application form for the Air Force. In September 1943, Joe knocked on the Halleys' door and persuaded his best friend, Bill Halley, to abandon his plans to become a doctor at university and join the Air Force with him (the RCAF offered quicker promotion than the Army!). A third friend, Larry Lawlor, enlisted with them and the three boys went to Montreal for their initial training. Before setting sail for England, they decided to have studio portrait photographs taken for posterity but only Larry had a clean shirt, which they passed from one to another as they were photographed. Obsessed with food on the ship across the Atlantic, they soon struck a deal with the cooks – if they peeled potatoes in the galley, they got bigger rations. Caught red-handed by an officer, they were hauled up for a lecture and reminded that: "sergeants don't peel potatoes". Thereafter, they were made to do submarine watch instead, Joe on starboard and Bill on port. Joe and Bill crewed up together and, after a spell in Liverpool and Scotland with their new crew (where they discovered they could use their rating tickets to get meals in restaurants.... food again!) went to Langar on 20 October 1944 and No. 5 LFS RAF Syerston on 17 December.

The family remember Joe's mother, Pauline, waking up and screaming in the night: "He's dead, Joe's dead". The telegram arrived the following day.

Joe is buried in Harrogate Stonefall Cemetery.

Bill Halley should have been in Lancaster LM308 with his crew on 29 January, but had a head-cold and went to bed early, having watched his crew-mates take off for their cross-country flight. He was told of the crash by officers in the morning and was understandably "pretty broken up" at the loss of his crew and friends. He transferred shortly afterwards to No. 6 Group Bomber Command. Bill, now 84 years old, lives in Cornwall, Ontario. Bill's place as rear-gunner that night was taken by Jasper Martin (see below).

Jasper Martin
Rear Gunner

Jasper was one of twelve children. He was not at all keen on his name ("he hated it" says his girlfriend, Molly) and was called "Tab" by everybody. The family lived at Castleford in Yorkshire; their father was a miner and their mother had died when Jasper was quite young. Jasper was a bright boy and attended Whitwood Technical and Mining College to train as a pit manager (he would have been the youngest pit manager in the area). He had a greyhound – also called Tab – which he assured the family might win some money one day (it didn't, according to his sister Nancy). Nancy remembers him as a "very willing person" who was much-loved by family and friends. Whenever he came home on leave it was Molly he went to see first. They went out together for eighteen months and Jasper always brought chocolate for her young nephew. Jasper's family always gave him an apple and an orange when he had to return to the air base from leave. Molly says Jasper was a "smashing lad" and that his last words to her before he returned to Syerston were: "Always remember that I love you".

It was Jasper's brother who came to tell her "our Tab's been killed in a crash". Nancy made the funeral arrangements and the family had to sign a letter promising the RAF padre that they would not open the coffin. Nancy sat by the coffin all night (she could not be sure her distraught father would not try to see his son for one last time). Jasper had been due to be the best man at Nancy's wedding the following month; she and her fiancé postponed the date until September. His coffin was borne in a horse-drawn hearse and he is buried in Castleford (Whitwood) Cemetery.

Jasper was singularly unlucky, having taken the place of Bill Halley, the regular rear-gunner in the crew of LM308, who was ill with a head-cold (see above).

Albert Mercer
Flight Engineer

Albert was one of five children; he had two brothers and two sisters. His father was a mainline steam train driver. Albert, recalls his sister Olive, was the "favourite" of his parents despite being the most trouble! His cousin Janice was living with her grandparents in Southport and remembers Sunday morning visits to Albert's home. He loved music and could memorise a tune before playing it "by ear" for his young cousins to dance to, "In the Mood" being a particular favourite. He was patient with children and had a lively personality, being "full of fun and life and mischief". His great passion was horses and he worked as a stable boy to finance his two ponies, which he competed on in local shows. He brought his crew mates Rathbone and Emerson home with him for what was to be his last Christmas, 1944. In one of his letters from Langar, Rathbone referred to Albert as "Bert" and describes him as a "good fellow" who "comes from Blackpool or some place nearby" but "I've forgotten the name of it and he's asleep now". Rathbone wrote that Albert had a nice home and "his people are nice". Albert had a Red Panther motorcycle, which was admired by others in his crew, and which he rode back to Syerston.

Olive returned home from work in bomb-devastated Liverpool on 30 January 1945 and recalls that, as she reached her parents' house, there were no lights on and she had a premonition that something was wrong. Her parents were sitting silently in the firelight and Billy, her youngest brother, who was sitting on the floor, said, "Albert's crashed".

Their father returned to work the following day and a young RAF officer came to discuss the return of Albert's body. The undertaker was a close family friend and repeated the official strict instructions not to open the coffin. The family was not told where or why Albert's Lancaster had crashed, and no one talked about the accident after the funeral.

Albert is buried in Southport (Duke Street) Cemetery.

Chapter Ten

CONCLUSION

The Allied bomber offensive in Europe cost over 500,000 civilian lives – men, women and children (some estimates say up to 800,000).

Of the 70,253 RAF airmen killed during the war, 55,573 were from Bomber Command. A further 8,403 bomber crewmen were injured. Nineteen Victoria Crosses were awarded to men in Bomber Command, ten of them for action seen in Lancasters. Bomber Command flew nearly 400,000 sorties during the war and well over a third of these were in Lancasters. Nearly 9,000 bombers, not just Lancasters, were lost throughout the conflict.

Over the following 65 years, the strategy of Bomber Command (and particularly of Harris, during his time as Commander-in-Chief) has attracted a significant degree of controversy and, even, outright condemnation from many quarters. Yet there cannot have been many Allied war leaders who, like him, had to prepare for a major battle virtually on a daily basis. The Allied bombing campaign had its roots in trying to weaken and defeat the Axis powers and was regarded as a just cause by many in Britain throughout the war. Harris died in 1984, aged 91, and for the rest of his life, he was saddened that "his boys" never got a Campaign medal of their own.

The more I learned about Bomber Command and its men, the greater the range of opinions I heard about their role, and their effect on the outcome of the war. What is not disputed by anyone is the bravery of the aircrews, who believed fervently – and rightly – that they were helping to turn the tide of war. This conviction was what drove them, night after night, to climb into those aircraft, and to confront unimaginable horrors over the continent.

As my own testament to their bravery, I wanted to portray something of what it was like for those crews – their training, their aircraft, and their camaraderie. I wanted to provide a backdrop for the tragic events here in Hoveringham and for how fourteen young men came to die in the fields in front of our house in January 1945.

I am indebted to all the former aircrew who have generously provided information and memories for this book, allowing me to pull back the curtain of time and take a better look at what is a defining era in our history. I was struck by the way they could describe something amusing, followed, almost in the same breath, by a heart-wrenchingly sad tale. These are men who, like all servicemen caught up in the front line of the war, learned the hard way how to deal with whatever life tossed at them. To those who say: "they don't make them like that any more," I would reply that, in fact, they do. Take a look at the young men (and women, now) who are facing their own, modern horrors in Afghanistan, and before that, in Iraq, Sierra Leone, Kosovo, to name a few.

The bomber stations, of which there are many locally, have largely returned to agriculture or been taken over by industry, although traces of concrete runways, dispersals, perimeter tracks and roads can still be discerned. A few of these airfields even retain their control towers, derelict and open to the elements, but the windows, which once watched countless bombers taking off and landing, are now empty and sightless.

RAF Syerston remains in daily use by the RAF, although in a much reduced capacity. If you stand beside its windswept and lonely boundary, the dispersals are clearly visible. Some are in the woods, overgrown with brambles around their edges but still identifiably circular. There are no ground crews or airmen waiting to get into their aircraft now, only the sound of birds and the wind in the trees, but if you stand for a moment and close your eyes, you can almost hear Merlin engines roaring into life around you.

I have tried to do justice to the memories that have been shared with me. The legacy of the airmen's courage – "the courage of the small hours" – as Harris himself put it, is the instant curiosity and unreserved admiration shown by people of all ages when the subject of Lancasters and Bomber Command is raised. We talk about "heroes" so readily these days; the word is applied in a million ways depending on the individual's perception of heroism.

To me, though, it is the young bomber crews, undergoing training and then flying nightly on hellish missions, who represent the ultimate in bravery and sacrifice: they are heroes.

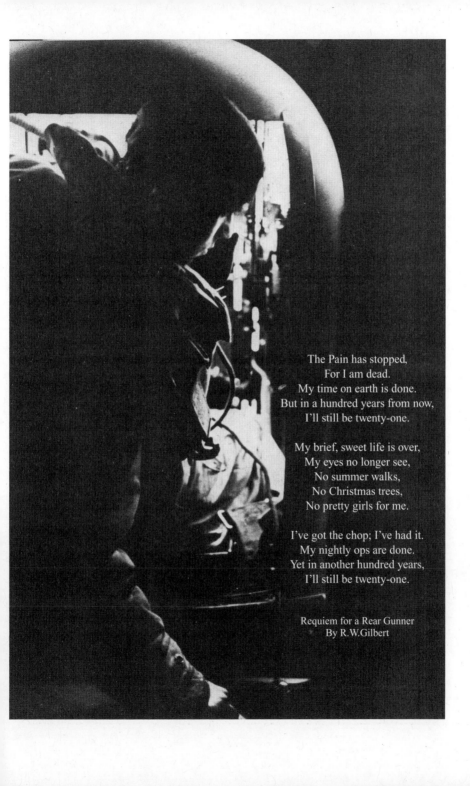

The Pain has stopped,
For I am dead.
My time on earth is done.
But in a hundred years from now,
I'll still be twenty-one.

My brief, sweet life is over,
My eyes no longer see,
No summer walks,
No Christmas trees,
No pretty girls for me.

I've got the chop; I've had it.
My nightly ops are done.
Yet in another hundred years,
I'll still be twenty-one.

Requiem for a Rear Gunner
By R.W.Gilbert

Bibliography

"The RAF at War"	Ralph Barker	(Time Life Books)
"Lancaster"	Leo McKinstry	John Murray
"The Most Dangerous Enemy"	Stephen Bungay	Aurum Press Ltd
"Hell on Earth"	Mel Rolfe	Grub Street, London
"Enemy Coast Ahead"	Guy Gibson, VC	Pan Books Ltd
"Bomber Offensive"	Sir Arthur Harris	Greenhill Books
"Action Stations"	Bruce Barrymore Halpenny	Patrick Stephens Ltd
"Lancaster Target"	Jack Currie	Goodall Publications Ltd
"Lancaster at War"	Brian Goulding/ Mike Garbett	Ian Allan Ltd
"Inferno"	Keith Lowe	Penguin Books
"Among the Dead Cities"	A.C.Grayling	Bloomsbury Publishing
"Bomber Command"	Max Hastings	Pan Books Ltd
"The Storm of War"	Andrew Roberts	Allen Lane